T0352539

THE
WITCH'S BOOK OF
POTIONS

About the Author

Michael Furie (Northern California) is the author of *Supermarket Sabbats, Spellcasting for Beginners, Supermarket Magic, Spellcasting: Beyond the Basics*, and more, all from Llewellyn Worldwide. A practicing Witch for more than twenty years, he is a priest of the Cailleach.

To Write to the Author

If you wish to contact the author or would like more information about this book, please write to the author in care of Llewellyn Worldwide Ltd. and we will forward your request. Both the author and publisher appreciate hearing from you and learning of your enjoyment of this book and how it has helped you. Llewellyn Worldwide Ltd. cannot guarantee that every letter written to the author can be answered, but all will be forwarded. Please write to:

Michael Furie
⁄ Llewellyn Worldwide
2143 Wooddale Drive
Woodbury, MN 55125-2989

Please enclose a self-addressed stamped envelope for reply, or $1.00 to cover costs. If outside the U.S.A., enclose an international postal reply coupon.

Many of Llewellyn's authors have websites with additional information and resources. For more information, please visit our website at http://www.llewellyn.com

MICHAEL FURIE

THE WITCH'S BOOK OF POTIONS

The Power of Bubbling Brews,
Simmering Infusions & Magical Elixirs

Llewellyn Publications | Woodbury, Minnesota

FIRST EDITION
Fourth Printing, 2023

Book design by Samantha Peterson
Cover design by Shannon McKuhen
Cover illustration by Eduardo Fuentes / Debut Art, Ltd.
Editing by Laura Kurtz
Interior art by Llewellyn Art Department

Llewellyn Publications is a registered trademark of Llewellyn Worldwide Ltd.

Library of Congress Cataloging-in-Publication Data
Names: Furie, Michael, author.
Title: The witch's book of potions : the power of bubbling brews, simmering
    infusions & magical elixirs / Michael Furie ; editing by Laura Kurtz.
Description: First edition. | Woodbury, Minnesota : Llewellyn Publications,
    [2021] | Includes bibliographical references and index. | Sum mary:
    "Pagan-focused book on potions and other related recipes"—Provided by
    publisher.
Identifiers: LCCN 2020047248 (print) | LCCN 2020047249 (ebook) | ISBN
    9780738764955 (paperback) | ISBN 9780738765037 (ebook)
Subjects: LCSH: Magic. | Witchcraft. | Formulas, recipes, etc. | Paganism.
Classification: LCC BF1621 .F873 2021 (print) | LCC BF1621 (ebook) | DDC
    133.4/3—dc23
LC record available at https://lccn.loc.gov/2020047248
LC ebook record available at https://lccn.loc.gov/2020047249

Llewellyn Publications
A Division of Llewellyn Worldwide Ltd.
2143 Wooddale Drive
Woodbury, MN 55125-2989
www.llewellyn.com

Printed in the United States of America

Other Books by Michael Furie

Spellcasting for Beginners (Llewellyn, 2012)

Supermarket Magic (Llewellyn, 2013)

Spellcasting Beyond the Basics (Llewellyn, 2016)

Supermarket Sabbats (Llewellyn, 2017)

To the Witches of the past, present, and future who have stirred the cauldrons, brewed the potions, and kept the magic alive; may it never be lost.

To my partner Drake Furie, for keeping me going through encouragement, love, and lots of coffee.

To my family, for the reassurance, support, and really good food.

To friends close and far away: Ty and Marco, thank you for all of the conversations, laughter, coffee, and really good cheesecake over the years.

To James and Andy, whether hanging out by the bay or up a mile high, thank you for being friends.

To Melanie Marquis, one of the brightest lights in the Witchy world, thank you for your friendship, kindness, and insight.

To my Llewellyn family: To Elysia Gallo, editor extraordinaire and unsung shero of so many authors. I can't sing, so I will say: we'd be nothing without you.

To Laura Kurtz, fabulous production editor who has saved me from myself on many occasions when I didn't even catch my mistake. I am always grateful. Many thanks to you.

To Kat Sanborn, wonderful publicist. Thank you for challenging me to try to overcome my fear of public speaking and my overall shyness and for the wonderful conversations at PantheaCon in days gone by.

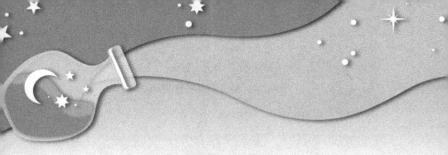

CONTENTS

Part 3
CC●))
BEYOND WATER:
OTHER MAGICAL MIXTURES

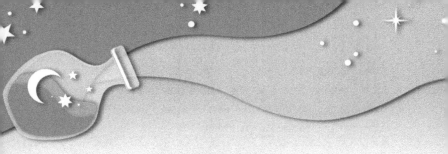

PREFACE

I feel compelled to state here that my scope for this work shall be primarily potions and brews that have been used by Witches—myself, those personally known to me, and those historically associated with what is generally understood as Witchcraft. I am making this point so as to avoid intentional cultural appropriation of others' practices, and neither do I wish to encourage further consumption of rare plants and other substances by contributing to any demand. Ayahuasca, for example, has gained greater notoriety in the United States in the last few years, but the brew has been a traditional part of spiritual practice for some of the tribes in the Amazonian basin for generations. Popularizing something increases the demand for it, which then increases the strain on the supply and potentially causes that supply to become endangered. We have seen this phenomenon with frankincense, sandalwood, and palo santo. Therefore, it will be my goal to reveal potion recipes that do not appropriate or endanger any culture or substance any more than would a regular trip to the supermarket.

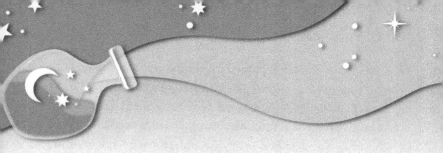

INTRODUCTION

When I was a kid, I used to "play witch." I would take a pot, water, and some cooking spices and stir together "potions" in the backyard. Unfortunately, I was foolhardy enough to actually taste some of these mixtures—they were the most unpleasant things I could ever imagine. (One involving seasoned salt and another with tons of curry powder come to mind.) Despite my early playtime pitfalls, I had some inner sense that potion making was somehow meant to be a part of my life. Eventually, I grew up and began practicing actual Witchcraft and my intuitive perception was fulfilled; I have indeed become very fond of potion and brew making. There is something so perfectly dramatic and innately magical about gathering various ingredients and combining them into a rich mixture of liquid; adding and stirring as fragrant steam rises from the bubbling cauldron.

I think what first piqued my interest even as a child with potion making were depictions of potion making—*Macbeth*'s "Witches" could be to blame, as could the Wicked Queen of Snow White; who can say? The image of Witches brewing up their potions in a cauldron over a fire is firmly implanted in our collective mindset. It has been a long-standing practice for Witches and other magical people to create homemade medicines, tonics, elixirs, potions, and other brews frequently in a cauldron. As much incorrect propaganda as has been spread about Witchcraft over the centuries, I have always deeply enjoyed those dramatized aspects that in fact turn out to be true.

Whether in a cast-iron cauldron set atop a bonfire, an enamel pot on the burner of a kitchen stove, or even in a cof-feepot, the power of a Witch's brew remains a potent, effective form of magical practice that anyone can engage in, regardless of spiritual path. I have always considered it strange that although the image of a Witch stirring a bubbling cauldron is so universal, actual practical information on the art was somewhat lacking. Plenty of works contain magical incense, oil, powder, ointment formulas, and even recipes for magical food and drinks, but there are relatively few with a primary focus of providing potion and brew mixtures. This book is my way of helping to fill that gap, so it contains dozens of traditional and modern concoctions. Potion and brew formulas will take the lead though a few recipes for oils, ointments, food, and so on are included.

NOTE: Both in my personal practice and in this book, I differentiate between potions and brews by using the term *potion* to refer exclusively to magically charged, water-based, edible, herb-infused, or boiled liquids and using the term *brew* for similar liquids that are inedible. For all the recipes found in this book, the rule applies: you can drink a potion (unless you are allergic to the ingredients) but do not drink a brew. And though the word "brew" is used, none of the recipes featured involve an actual fermentation process. As the word is used in this book, "brew" is meant to be of similar usage to that of brewing tea, essentially a steeping process.

Part 1
BACKGROUND
AND BASICS

This part of the book details all of the essential preliminary information on potion and brew making, from choosing the right cooking vessel to magically empowering the ingredients so that the finished creation is fully charged with your energy and intention. In this way, we can first lay the groundwork and then fully dive into the recipes. The earliest potions were bubbled up over a fire in the most magical of vessels—the cauldron. Even though we live in the modern era, cauldrons are still an integral part of many a Witch's craft. As a tool for brewing, in my opinion, its power is unequaled. Cauldrons are steeped in symbolism, secrets, and lore; an understanding of their place in magical cookery is a great thing to explore. After we look at the magical basics, there will be a brief overview of cauldrons and their symbolism, history, and magic.

To begin is a short overview of some of the main points of magical practice and some of the theory on how magic works. There will also be some information on each of the steps in potion making and technicalities such as the difference in how to use water to extract the properties of herbs versus the process of water extraction from tougher plant materials such as roots. Let us start the journey with the primary steps in the processes of both potion making and general magical work and empowerment.

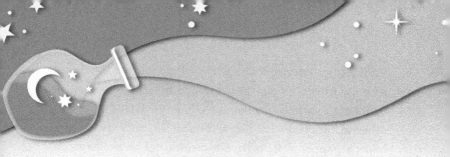

Chapter 1
BREW MAKING
AND MAGICAL BASICS

On the surface, brews sound easy enough to make; some herbs, a little water, a pot, heat until bubbling, and cackle as desired ... but there is a little more to it than that. First, all the herbs and other ingredients should be gathered beforehand and ideally be placed in individual cups or bowls (like on a TV cooking show) so that each can be charged with intent before being added into the collective energy of the brew. When the recipes in this book were created, each herb, flower, and other ingredient was included for specific reasons, primarily to extract its unique essences. In magic such as brewing, the ingredients are chosen based on two criteria: correspondence and alignment. Though there are other meanings, *correspondence* in a magical context can be defined as two or more things sharing a close similarity or connection, such as a seashell used as a way to draw in the influence of the oceans. *Alignment* can be defined as an arrangement of things in relation to each other in order to establish a connection, such as empowering a poppet doll to have a magical effect on a specific person. Correspondences can be used to help form alignments. When ingredients have natural correspondences to a magical goal and are combined together, their innate affinities can be enhanced by empowering them with a specific intent. This action charges them with the goal's power and binds the ingredients together in alignment.

Process of Empowerment

From the simplest blessing to elaborate ritual spellwork, magic must rely on the process of empowerment. As it applies specifically to potion and brew making, the empowerment process usually consists of gathering each of the ingredients for the brew (ideally in separate containers) and holding each ingredient in your hand (or holding your hand over it if it's too large) while focusing on your magical goal. Mentally send the energy of your intention into the ingredient and visualize it mingling with the essence already present. Will that all the energies within the ingredient shall come into alignment with your goal. Once each of the ingredients is charged in this way, they can be combined into a single vessel to await transfer to the liquid or you can leave them in their containers so that they can be added to the brew one at a time which adds a lovely "eye of newt, toe of frog" witchiness to the process. The desired amount of liquid (usually water) is measured into the pot and can then be charged by holding your hands over it and willing your intention into the water with the added condition that any energy not in harmony with your goal will be neutralized. From there, unless otherwise instructed, the liquid is heated until it just begins to form bubbles on the bottom of the pot, just before boiling point. The other ingredients are added at this stage, the pot is removed from the heat, and the mixture is stirred. It is usually a good idea to have a special spoon solely reserved for magical use; wooden spoons work well though they absorb some of the essence from the herbs. You can hold your hands over the pot and send energy into the brew, further charging it and affirming once more that the completed mixture shall manifest your intention. Finally, cover with the lid and let the herbs and liquid steep for ten to fifteen minutes to allow everything to infuse (and the brew to cool and herbs to settle to the bottom), then strain into a cup or use as directed. This method is known as an *infusion* and is the primary process used in this book's recipes. The light plant materials are steeped in the heated liquid to extract their oils, vitamins, and other compounds into the liquid. A second method, known as a *decoction* is similar but is used for heavier plant materials such as bark, roots, and thick seeds. These tougher materials usually need to be boiled for anywhere from ten minutes to half an hour or longer in order to fully extract their mineral salts and other properties into the liquid. Though most of the recipes contained in this book will not require overly elaborate or intense preparation, in the cases of potions with a blend of both delicate herbs and heavy roots or barks, a two-step process may be required and will be noted in such cases in the instructions.

For the most part, the process of potion making is simple and enjoyable. If you wish to create a small ritual around the making and use of a potion, it can help to focus the magic. Taking care to enhance each step of the process with your intention is a powerful magical boost. To truly immerse yourself in the process, a short spell chant can be created to seal in your specific intention for the finished potion or brew and this chant can be repeated as the ingredients are added to the cauldron. It does add a great deal of Witchy flair to chant and add each ingredient one at a time, stirring it into the liquid with each addition; adding, stirring, and chanting, it all helps to build the energy of the finished product. Using the Boundary Ward Banishing Brew (found on page 79) as an example, a simple chant could be created that addresses the overall intention for its use such as, "Herbs of power, bring all harm to an end; magical brew, protect and defend!" This can be repeated as each ingredient is added. A longer, more complex chant could be created instead that addresses the individual powers of each of the ingredients in a fashion similar to that of the Witches in *Macbeth* such as, "Guardian nettle, stinging briar, lend your power to me this hour; mighty mullein, candlewick plant, protection from harmful beasts now grant; magical onion, great strength do you wield, from evil forces your power will shield; into this water, my Witch's brew, merging your energy, magic imbued!" This of course could be said in stages as each ingredient is added and stirred into the water. This type of procedure can be created for any of the potion or brew recipes in this book, or any other book for that matter, to add energy, atmosphere, and a more specific focus to the magical intention. This personalizes the process so that it becomes your own. After the potion or brew has been created, all that is left is to use it as directed. Of course, since "use as directed" is a bit vague, a look at the primary ways to make use of brews (and/or potions) in practical magic is warranted.

What to Do with That Brew?

Despite the vivid stereotype of the Witch stirring up potions in an enormous cauldron bubbling over a fire, the practice seems to have fallen out of fashion in modern times, save for some health tonic and herbal tea recipes scattered here and there online and in books. Most of the legends surrounding the practice focus on nefarious uses of potions such as "love potions" or the creation of poisonous mixtures, but I have spent years collecting, creating, experimenting with, and using potions and brews for a variety of purposes that are all free of such unethical or disturbing intentions. Just because you won't find a mixture to turn someone into a "love slave" or transform those annoying politicians into toads doesn't mean that there aren't plenty of magical secrets to be uncovered. Actually, a few words of caution are in order here regarding the use of these recipes and herb work in general. The standard warning against using anything contained herein as medical advice applies, as does seeking professional medical help in the case of illness or injury as the first step and only relying on any alternative healing options as a supplement. Another important point: if any of the recipes are meant to be ingested, make sure that they do not contain anything to which you are allergic. If allergies are a concern, either substitute the unsafe ingredient with something better suited or skip the recipe entirely.

Aside from the cautions, there are quite a few uses for magical brews and potions depending on type and intentions. Some are used as an anointing liquid in a similar fashion as magical oils, applied either directly on the skin or on objects or charms to charge them with energy. In other cases, a brew may be used to asperge (sprinkle) an area in order to cleanse it of any unsettling vibrations or to protect it from harm. Another excellent means of using a brew is as the liquid in a bottle spell. Witch bottles (or spell bottles) have a long and colorful history behind them; originally used as protective devices or to destroy or reflect a curse back to its sender, nowadays their uses have expanded to a full range of magical intentions. In the type of bottle magic I use, a variety of ingredients can be gathered together and placed inside a container, after which usually a liquid of some sort is poured into it to bind the ingredients together and activate the magic. In this work, a specially made brew becomes a valuable magical catalyst. In work such as divinatory scrying, the concoction can be used as more of a magical receptor or reservoir.

Using any type of liquid in spellwork almost automatically brings to mind the idea of elemental water magic, which indeed potions and brews can be used to create. What's more, they can also be used to draw upon the other elements of fire, earth, air, and spirit. In fact, depending upon their composition, some of these recipes can aid in the summoning of not only elemental forces but spiritual and divine forces and beings too. While there is a wide range of uses for these magical mixtures, the way their power is created is rooted in the same foundational principles as all magical practices.

My personal definition of magic is as follows: the science and process of projecting emotionally and intellectually charged energy into the spiritual plane in order to manifest change in the physical world. And while this definition may explain how I view magic, it does not even begin to explain how the process works. I like to think of it with a scientific(ish) mindset and feel that the power that underlies all magical work can be efficiently used through consistently employing three key factors during any and all spellwork; thinking, feeling, and willing. If we look at magical energy in a similar fashion to radio waves, we can imagine ourselves as both a transmitter and receiver of these waves. Casting a spell can be seen as though we are playing a song that touches us deeply.

When that perfect song comes on the car radio, a flood of memories and emotions well up within, and you just want to turn it all the way up and blast it for the entire world to hear; it's a lot like casting a spell. The station or channel on the radio is set to a certain frequency, akin to the type of magical intention you are harnessing (love, money, healing, etc.) in that different stations play different genres of music (rap, rock, country, and so forth). The song is both our power and our emotional connection to our intention. The stronger the intention and emotional connection are felt, the greater the spell's power and effect. The strength of both our intention (thinking) and emotional connection (feeling) merge and form our ability to project the magic outward to its destination. This is the "turning it up full blast" part wherein the volume or amplitude of the energy is projected through our sheer force of will. All of this magical energy can be harnessed in spellwork of all kinds and can be used to charge up our brews and potions. Before we can empower our potions, we first have to brew them up somehow. The following chapter explores the different types of pots, kettles, and cauldrons that can be used in this process, with a bit of history thrown in for good measure.

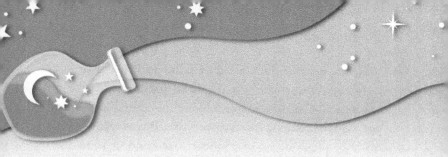

Chapter 2
CAULDRONS, KETTLES, AND OTHER BREWING OPTIONS

A cauldron is an object that both symbolizes and can contain great power. Though potions and other brews can be created in vessels besides cauldrons, they are *the* tool most universally associated with these magical concoctions. Potion pot, offering receptacle, ritual hearth—cauldrons have many uses. Many of the associated practices go back centuries in one form or another, but why a cauldron as opposed to some other implement? To answer that question, we have to look to history. This is not to say that one must have a "proper" cauldron of such and such a type in order to create brews and potions. Glass or enamel pots work well, but no book about Witches' brews would be complete without a look at the original vessels for creation.

Once upon a time, at some point in the late Bronze/ early Iron Age, people began to create cauldrons. A cauldron can basically be defined as a usually round and large metal pot used for cooking over an open fire. These creations were made of plates of copper, bronze, iron, and/or sometimes silver, usually riveted together to form a complete vessel. The cauldrons of old were apparently used for all sorts of practical purposes, from bathing children, to dyeing and washing fabrics, to cooking large amounts of food, to holding assorted items. They were also used ceremonially either to hold offerings to various deities or as the offerings themselves. Ancient cauldrons have been unearthed from bogs, rivers, wells, and burial chambers that appear to have been used as part of ritual. Four notable discoveries are the Battersea Cauldron, the Chiseldon Cauldrons, the Basal Cauldrons, and, of course, the Gundestrup Cauldron.

Battersea Cauldron

The Battersea Cauldron was recovered from the River Thames in the year 1861. It is now on display in the British Museum in London. Believed to date from the late Bronze/early Iron Age (ca. 800–700 BCE), it is constructed of seven bronze sheets that were curved and riveted together; it also has two handles on the top.

Chiseldon Cauldrons

In 2004, twelve cauldrons dating from the Iron Age were uncovered in a pit, along with two cow skulls in Chiseldon, England. They were apparently constructed of iron as well as copper alloy and were believed to have been gathered together and buried in a ritual context.

Basal Cauldrons

In 2010, a large burial pit was uncovered in Basal Gasfabrik, Switzerland, in which two Iron Age cauldrons were discovered among other metal and ceramic vessels, and are thought to have been buried as part of a ritual activity, similar to the cauldrons found in Britain.

Gundestrup Cauldron

Arguably the most famous of the ancient vessels, this cauldron was unearthed from a peat bog in the area of Gundestrup, Denmark, in 1891. It is thought that this cauldron dates from 150 BCE to 400 CE, at some point in the early Roman Iron Age. It is constructed in silver and features very detailed decorations. Some of the images depicted on the cauldron's surface include human faces, animals such as lions and deer, and what is believed to be an image of Cernunnos, the Horned God. The vessel was taken apart, and each of its pieces was placed in the bog centuries ago in an apparent ritual act. Though it was found in Denmark, it is thought to be of Celtic and/or Thracian origin, possibly created in an area where both peoples lived closely, such as in southwest Romania or northwest Bulgaria. The silverwork is considered to be in the style of the Thracians of the time, whereas the images on the cauldron plates are very Celtic in appearance. This cauldron is currently on display in the National Museum of Denmark in Copenhagen.

Usage: Modern and Ancient

Originally, a cauldron was a vital item, a multipurpose vessel essential to a household for cooking, cleaning, healing, and warmth; it was the oven, cooking pot, medicine maker, wash tub, radiant heater, and so on, making it indispensable. The earliest cauldrons seem to have been made primarily of copper or bronze (and sometimes stone or clay), but today's cauldrons are most often constructed from cast iron. This is not a new practice; they didn't call it the Iron Age for nothing! It just shows that the cauldron as a real, physical, practical, and spiritual tool actually predates the use of iron, the metal for which it is most commonly associated. It is good to know that even though the iron cauldron has been the dominant form since roughly the Middle Ages, it is not the original or only "valid" form of cauldron in existence.

Though in our modern era, the cauldron and Witch are practically inseparable and it is rare to find one in a so-called normal setting, historically cauldrons were important items for a household to have akin to our kitchen stoves. If you walked into someone's kitchen today and the stove was missing, it would be as odd as a household minus a cauldron would've been in ancient times. The standard legend goes that during the Burning Times of persecution, most Witchcraft tools had to be ordinary household items given a special purpose. It is said that this is how things such as the athame (knife), broom, chalice, and so on became part of a Witch's magic; because everybody already had these things in their homes, their use was not an obvious sign of Witchcraft. Whether that is true or not, I cannot say; in any case, it is only partially true of the cauldron. Though in those days it was an important household item, cauldrons have been steeped in magical lore from their very beginnings.

Far from being merely a human invention, since ancient times it has been believed that there exists cauldrons of divine magical power, owned by deities and capable of profound supernatural manifestations such as providing an inexhaustible supply of food or even reviving the deceased. In much of the modern craft, it is customary to view the cauldron as symbolic of the Goddess. The typical round, pot-bellied shape is said to symbolize the womb and creation, and the three legs upon which the cauldron stands can serve as reminders of a threefold nature to some goddess(es); maidens, mothers, and crones; birth, life, death; and so on. This concept too stretches back through history in part, as cauldrons have nearly always been associated with the divine feminine. Since the cauldron was so integral to a comfortable existence, it was seen as a great provider and equated to the earth and sea, the great providers of nature. This divine connection is the "why" of cauldron use; though another vessel could be used, none are as rich in symbolism, lore and historical use as the cauldron. Despite their ideal connection to magical brewing, it is not always feasible or practical to have a cauldron bubbling out in the forest or even on the kitchen stove, so there are a few more modern options to consider.

Granted, if you already have a preferred vessel (or two) for making potions and brews and it is properly seasoned and ready, you can skip ahead to chapter 2. If, on the other hand, you would like some tips on how to find the best cauldron (including some very important safeguards), how to care for your cauldron depending on its type, and what to use as an alternative brewing vessel, this chapter is for you. I have observed some curious phenomena when it comes to modern-day cauldrons; firstly, so many of the ones offered for sale are not food safe! Secondly, a great many of them cost quite a bit of money, especially considering their size. Lastly, the symbolic importance of the cauldron seems to have far outpaced the practical uses for the vessel, save as a receptacle for fire.

There really isn't a problem in using a cauldron exclusively as an incense burner or to hold spell candles and offerings during ritual, but if you intend to cook with one, it has to be designated as "food grade" in its construction. Unless it is specifically stated at the time of purchase that the cauldron is made of food-safe materials, it is unwise to use one to prepare anything edible. Some cauldrons are coated with inedible oils and finishes, and others are painted with potentially leaded paint. Vintage cauldrons can have a varied history and are most often best reserved for symbolic purposes. Even when getting the right kind of pot, it still needs to be properly prepared before its first use (at least as a cooking vessel). Iron cauldrons have to be seasoned in the same manner as cast-iron pans in order to give the metal a protective cooking surface. Without seasoning, anything cooked or brewed in cast iron will have a metallic taste to it and the vessel will be much more vulnerable to rust.

Seasoning cast iron is a simple enough process provided that the item you are working with is small enough to fit in your oven or a lidded outdoor grill.

★ Seasoning a Cast-Iron Cauldron ★

Items Needed

Oven or outdoor grill

Cauldron

Paper towels

Wax paper (optional)

2 large cookie sheets (for the oven method)

Aluminum foil (for the oven method)

Scouring pad

Dish cloth

Vegetable shortening, coconut oil, or lard

The first step is to use the scouring pad to scrub both the inside and outside of the cauldron to remove any debris or any factory-added coating on the surface. This scouring only needs to be done once unless the cauldron has been left to rust and would need to be re-seasoned from scratch again. After it has been thoroughly scrubbed, wash the pot in warm water *without* soap. Do not use soap to clean cast iron—especially if it is unseasoned—as the metal is porous and can absorb some of the soap which will not only mess up the finish but can also leach a soapy taste into anything prepared in the cauldron. Incidentally, using soap to wash cast iron is generally frowned upon because it can strip the season-coating. Simply wash the cauldron in warm water with a sponge and dry thoroughly. After it has been scoured and rinsed, dry the cauldron with a soft cloth. Preheat the oven to 350 degrees Fahrenheit (or the grill, if using). Line the cookie sheets with the foil and place one on the lowest rack in the oven to catch the oil drippings. Use a piece of wax paper to wipe the entire surface of the cauldron with the shortening, inside and out including the lid if there is one. Next, place the cauldron and lid upside down in the oven or grill. This will keep any melted shortening from pooling in the bottom of the pot, which would create a sticky, unusable mess. Bake the cauldron and lid for an hour. I've never had a problem with it becoming smoky, but as a general precaution, if using the indoor oven method, turn on the hood vent fan and open a nearby window if needed.

After the hour has passed, turn off the oven and remove the cauldron and lid using oven mitts as they will be quite hot. Set them on the clean cookie sheet right side up. Crumple up some of the paper towels and use them to soak up any excess oil that has pooled in the bottom of the pot while it cools. Once the metal has cooled for at least fifteen minutes or so, carefully wipe down the inside and outside of the cauldron and lid to remove any extra residue being careful not to burn yourself. Allow them to cool completely before working with or storing them. If there is any stickiness on the metal, it needs to be heated further. You can repeat the steps from coating it again with shortening through the baking, cooling, and wipe down steps in order to give the metal a proper finish.

Once properly seasoned, the cauldron can be used for cooking, brewing, and potion making. It can also serve as a fire receptacle or censer, but avoid leaving ashes or wax from candles in there for long periods of time, as they can wear away the seasoning. Cooking fatty foods in cast iron helps to strengthen the protective coating (remember to clean out the excess oil each time), while cooking acidic things in it will gradually strip away seasoning, leaving the cauldron susceptible to rust and corrosion. In my own practice, I have a food-grade cast-iron cauldron that I use all the time. Its seasoning holds up pretty well despite heavy usage. To be on the safe side, I do a simple re-season (the process of coating with shortening, baking, and wiping clean) once a year in wintertime. Not only is winter the perfect time to protect the cast iron from moisture but it is also a great way to warm up a cold kitchen. Again, I must stress the importance of making certain that a cauldron is food safe, as seasoning an unsafe one will not remove the potential danger. As far as cast-iron cauldron use for making something edible, it is usually best to purchase a new one so you know what you are getting. Unfortunately, the same warning applies to the number one alternative to a cauldron, the enamel pot.

Modern commercially made enamel pots are generally regarded as safe, but some imported pieces of both enamel and ceramic cookware have levels of lead and/or cadmium that can leach into food. So for safety's sake, it is best to avoid cheap, imported, or vintage enamelware or ceramic pots.

Additionally, if the enamel coating is chipped or cracked, it is best to replace it so as not to risk any toxic exposure.[1] Another alternative to the cast-iron cauldron is a copper pot. Copper cauldrons are sometimes available as well, but a few precautions are needed here too. Ingredients that are too acidic can react with the copper and cause the metal to leach into what's prepared inside it. Additionally, it is important to keep the copper tarnish free as the green corrosion is toxic. Personally, I like copper cauldrons and cookware, but for the continuous practical use in brew making, I like to use something a bit more durable and worry-free.

If you wish to avoid the problems posed by metallic options altogether, many people have chosen tempered glass cookware as their main go-to for potion and brew making. This is a pretty safe alternative to cauldron use: modern glass cookware is considered inert and should not leach any chemicals into food and, if made of tempered glass, can usually withstand high heat. The only precautions to take here are making sure to avoid rapid temperature shifts (don't take a hot pot and run it under cold water or set it directly on a cold countertop) and to have a new pot specifically designated for magical use. It is best to have one vessel for magical work that is not mixed in with your usual cookware not only to keep

---

1. "The safe use of cookware," The Government of Canada. Last modified March 2015. https://www.canada.ca/en/health-canada/services /household-products/safe-use-cookware.html.

a sense of magic but also to make sure that food isn't altered with any residues that may linger in the pot.

Another definitely modern option is a coffeepot used for making your brew. This method feels a bit less magical to my mind, but there is no denying it is a practical way of brewing. It is still recommended that a separate coffee maker be obtained solely for magical use if possible. If you decide to upgrade to a new coffee maker, it would be good to reserve the old one (as long as it works) for a potion maker. The creation of brews in a coffee maker is quite easy to do: gather the herbs and other ingredients, place them in the filter just as you would ground coffee, fill the reservoir with the desired amount of water, and hit the "on" button. The coffee maker will create the potion or brew with a minimum of fuss. Remember to only use water in the reservoir. If other liquids are needed for a brew, add them into the coffeepot after the water heating and brewing are complete.

Part 2
MAGICAL POTIONS
AND BREWS

Toil? Trouble? Well perhaps, but I like to think that there is a great deal to enjoy about the process of potion and brew making and their use. It is such a part of the Witch's heritage and a great deal of practical magic can be achieved through the use of a good potion or brew, no lizard legs or bat wings required. Each of the recipes presented under the "potion" heading are created using only edible ingredients and are safe to consume as long as no one has an allergy to any of the ingredients. If an allergy is present, either avoid that recipe entirely or make a reasonable substitution of the problem ingredient. It is also wise to avoid the use of any potion during pregnancy; some herbs—particularly hyssop, mugwort, and wormwood—could create problems or reactions. It is also important to avoid any use of essential oils in any potion making: we aren't meant to ingest essential oils due to their usually highly concentrated form and they can cause digestive issues or allergic reactions even in people who have not previously shown any sensitivity to the oils' herbal form.

Even though potions are edible recipes, not every ingredient will be easy to obtain. The recipes given under the heading "Brews" are not meant to be ingested but instead have other uses such as anointing, sprinkling, divining, and so on. Since a lot of my work and two of my books have been centered upon herbs and supplies that can be obtained from the supermarket, I will place an asterisk (*) by the names of each recipe that are entirely "supermarket ready."

One bit of caution: though every effort has been made to ensure that the flavors of the edible recipes found in this book are palatable, not every potion is going to taste great. This is unavoidable in some cases, since it is the ingredients' energy which is of greatest importance. Additionally, some of the older recipes are given as I have learned them and may include rare ingredients. In such cases, I have offered reasonable substitutions so that they can be made without further endangering rare plants.

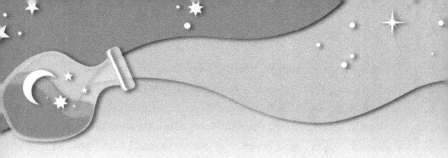

Chapter 3
ASTROLOGICAL AND
PLANETARY RECIPES

Our first foray into the practical magic of potions will be a walk through the zodiac and a flight through the solar system. First, the basics; in the field of astrology, each of the planets in our solar system (as well as some of the larger asteroids, our moon, and the sun) correspond to different aspects of our personalities and lives and are linked to one or more of the twelve signs of the zodiac. The zodiac or "circle of animals" is a grouping of constellations that are said to rule or at least influence the overall course of our lives through the interplay of planetary orbits and rotations which appear to occur (from our vantage point) within the range of those constellations. When each of us is born, all the different zodiacal happenings occurring in that instant are said to reveal what our strengths, weaknesses, and general temperaments are likely to be. Whichever zodiac sign the sun is passing through at the time we are born is said to be our "sun sign" and this is considered to be a major influence over our lives. I was born in mid-August and am therefore a Leo, as this was where the sun was passing when I was born. My book, *Spellcasting: Beyond the Basics,* contains much more detailed descriptions of astrological theory and associations; I won't repeat that information in full here, but more than enough guidance will be given.

Among the myriad correspondences attributed to herbs, flowers, roots, and so on are planetary and astrological associations that give us a greater understanding of how the individual planets relate to the greater macrocosm of life. That energetic interplay is the underlying basis for the creation of and use of these potions. Each recipe is crafted to enhance the most beneficial qualities of each zodiac sign as well as to draw in the planetary energies with suggested uses for their power provided. Though these potions are designed for their specific signs, they can be used by every sign to aid whichever quality they are crafted to enhance. Simply drink them to absorb their power.

Zodiac Sign Potion Recipes

The best place to start is at the beginning of the zodiac and so I will start with the potion for the sign of Aries.

Aries
(March 21 to April 19)

The powerful sign of Aries is the initiator of the season of spring. Those born under this sign are strong individuals gifted with endurance but who must caution against impulsiveness.

Keywords: Passion, action, force, strength

★ Aries Power Potion ★

Items Needed

  2 cups water

  1 tablespoon dried rosemary

  1 tablespoon dried nettle leaves

  3 cinnamon sticks, broken in half

  4 tablespoons blackberry jam (or ¼ cup blackberry juice)

  1 teaspoon vanilla extract

Heat the water on the stove and add the rosemary, nettle, and cinnamon (following the "Process of Empowerment" on page 8), charging the potion with the desire to enhance and reveal the best qualities of Aries. After the potion has steeped, stir in the jam or juice and add the vanilla. Strain through a sieve (if desired) into a cup and drink.

This potion can be drunk whenever an extra boost of strength and energy is needed for those born under the sign of Aries, and it can also be used by those of any sign to aid in endurance and increased willpower.

Taurus
(April 20 to May 20)

Taurus is the sign that is the embodiment of the season of spring and the power of earth in its active form. Those born under this sign are steadfast and reliable but must guard against stubbornness.

Keywords: Stability, possessions, tenacity

★ Taurus Power Potion* ★

Items Needed

    1 cup water

    ¼ cup mashed strawberries

    1 teaspoon dried spearmint (or two sprigs fresh)

    1 teaspoon dried sage

    1 teaspoon dried thyme

    1 cup apple juice

Heat the water on the stove and add the next four ingredients (following the "Process of Empowerment" on page 8), charging the potion with the desire to "enhance and reveal the best qualities of Taurus." After the potion has steeped, strain through a sieve and mix it with a cup of apple juice. Drink as desired.

This potion can be drunk whenever an extra boost of strength and stability is needed for those born under the sign of Taurus, and it can also be used by those of any sign to aid in endurance, determination, and decision-making.

Gemini
(May 21 to June 20)

This is a zodiac sign of change. It is the sign that drifts away from the season of spring, readying things for the next season. People born under the sign of Gemini are said to be born communicators and have bright, inquisitive natures but must beware of any tendency toward being emotionally cold or detached.

Keywords: Communication, learning, strategizing

★ Gemini Power Potion ★

Items Needed

    2 cups water

    2 tablespoons dried lavender

    2 tablespoons dried marjoram

Heat the water on the stove and add the lavender and marjoram (following the "Process of Empowerment" on page 8), charging the potion with the desire to enhance and reveal the best qualities of Gemini. After the potion has steeped, strain through a sieve and drink as desired.

This potion can be drunk whenever an extra boost of strength and energy is needed for those born under the sign of Gemini, and it can also be used by those of any sign to aid in enhanced communication and reasoning abilities.

Cancer
(June 21 to July 22)

This sign is the initiator of the season of summer. People born under this sign are sensitive, nurturing, and compassionate but must caution against a tendency toward moodiness.

Keywords: Home, protection, nurturing, mother

★ Cancer Power Potion* ★

Items Needed

    1 cup water

    3 bay leaves

    ½ teaspoon dried tarragon

    ½ teaspoon lemon zest

    1 cup grape juice

Heat the water on the stove and add the next three ingredients (following the "Process of Empowerment" on page 8), charging the potion with the desire to enhance and reveal the best qualities of Cancer. After the potion has steeped, strain through a sieve and mix with a cup of grape juice. Drink as desired.

This potion can be drunk whenever an extra boost of strength and energy is needed for those born under the sign of Cancer, and it can also be used by anyone of any sign to aid in protection, nurturing, growth, and lunar power.

Leo
(July 23 to August 22)

This sign is the embodiment of the season of summer. Strong-willed and determined, Leos must guard against becoming vain or excessively prideful.

Keywords: Pride, loyalty, strength, children

★ Leo Power Potion ★

Items Needed

2 cups water

1 tablespoon chamomile (or 2 chamomile tea bags)

1 tablespoon peppermint (or 2 peppermint tea bags)

1 teaspoon rosemary

1 teaspoon eyebright

Pinch cloves

Heat the water on the stove and add the next four ingredients (following the "Process of Empowerment" on page 8), charging the potion with the desire to enhance and reveal the best qualities of Leo. After the potion has steeped, add the pinch of cloves, strain through a sieve, and drink as desired.

This potion can be drunk whenever an extra boost of strength and energy is needed for those born under the sign of Leo, and it can also be used by anyone of any sign to aid in determination, increased self-esteem, and confidence.

♍

Virgo
(August 23 to September 21)

The sign of Virgo is an adaptable one and it brings on the changes necessary to move away from summer and on to the next season. Virgos are adaptable, conscientious, and detail-oriented but need to curb a tendency toward being nitpicky or pedantic.

Keywords: Health, work, service, pets

★ Virgo Power Potion ★

Items Needed

    2 cups water

    1 tablespoon lavender

    1 tablespoon fennel

    ¼ teaspoon cardamom

    2 teaspoons licorice root

Heat the water on the stove and add the remaining ingredients (following the "Process of Empowerment" on page 8), charging the potion with the desire to enhance and reveal the best qualities of Virgo. After the potion has steeped, strain through a sieve and drink as desired.

This potion can be drunk whenever an extra boost of strength and energy is needed for those born under the sign of Virgo, and it can also be used by anyone of any sign to aid in boosting health, strategic and critical thinking, and organization.

Libra
(September 22 to October 22)

The sign of Libra initiates the season of autumn. People born under this sign are warm, friendly, and usually talkative but may have a tendency to be indecisive.

Keywords: Justice, partnerships, marriage, balance

★ Libra Power Potion ★

Items Needed

    2 cups water

    2 tablespoons mint (spearmint, peppermint, or a blend)

    1 tablespoon rose petals (clean and pesticide free)

    1 tablespoon thyme

Heat the water on the stove and add the remaining ingredients (following the "Process of Empowerment" on page 8), charging the potion with the desire to enhance and reveal the best qualities of Libra. After the potion has steeped, strain through a sieve and drink as desired.

This potion can be drunk whenever an extra boost of strength and energy is needed for those born under the sign of Libra, and it can also be used by anyone of any sign to aid in balance, matters of fairness, communication in partnerships and friendships, and artistic pursuits.

Scorpio
(October 23 to November 21)

This is the sign that is the embodiment of the season of autumn. Scorpio is a powerful sign that has an unparalleled ability to focus and transcend obstacles but should guard against a tendency toward obsessiveness.

Keywords: Sex, intensity, death, past lives

★ Scorpio Power Potion ★

Items Needed

2 cups water

1 tablespoon basil

1 tablespoon nettle

1 teaspoon catnip

1 small piece horseradish (dime-sized or smaller)

Heat the water on the stove and add the next three ingredients (following the "Process of Empowerment" on page 8), charging the potion with the desire to "enhance and reveal the best qualities of Scorpio." While the potion is cooling, add the piece of horseradish. After the potion has steeped, strain through a sieve and drink as desired.

This potion can be drunk whenever an extra boost of strength and energy is needed for those born under the sign of Scorpio, and it can also be used by anyone of any sign to aid in focus, drive, sexuality, past life work, investigation, and overcoming obstacles.

Sagittarius
(November 22 to December 20)

This is the sign that breaks down the energy of autumn in preparation for the coming of winter. Sagittarius people tend to be bright, optimistic and usually have a great love of travel and/or higher learning. However, they should caution against being too detached or aloof.

Keywords: Travel, religion, education, philosophy, spontaneity

★ Sagittarius Power Potion ★

Items Needed

> 2 cups water
>
> 1 tablespoon sage
>
> 1 tablespoon dandelion root
>
> 1 teaspoon chicory
>
> ¼ teaspoon nutmeg

Heat the water on the stove and add the remaining ingredients (following the "Process of Empowerment" on page 8), charging the potion with the desire to "enhance and reveal the best qualities of Sagittarius." After the potion has steeped, strain through a sieve and drink as desired.

This potion can be drunk whenever an extra boost of strength and energy is needed for those born under the sign of Sagittarius, and it can also be used by anyone of any other sign to aid in matters of justice, learning, religious study, philosophical pondering, and travel planning.

♑

Capricorn
(December 21 to January 19)

The sign of Capricorn initiates the season of winter. Those of this sign are determined and goal-oriented but must guard against being too rigid or cold.

Keywords: Ambition, reputation, authority

★ Capricorn Power Potion ★

Items Needed

    2 cups water

    1 tablespoon mullein

    1 tablespoon chopped beet

    5 black cherries, pitted and mashed

    1 teaspoon dandelion root (dried)

Heat the water on the stove and add the remaining ingredients (following the "Process of Empowerment" on page 8), charging the potion with the desire to enhance and reveal the best qualities of Capricorn. After the potion has steeped, strain through a sieve and drink as desired.

This potion can be drunk whenever an extra boost of strength and energy is needed for those born under the sign of Capricorn, and it can also be used by anyone of any sign to aid in establishing or maintaining composure, reserve, and authority, or for boosting ambition.

Aquarius
(January 20 to February 18)

Aquarius is the sign that is the embodiment of the season of winter. Those born during this time are frequently gifted with a sharp mind and keen insights. Though rather future-oriented, Aquarians should be wary of a tendency toward overlooking details in pursuit of the big picture.

Keywords: Society, community, innovation, activism, insight

★ Aquarius Power Potion* ★

Items Needed

2 cups water

1 tablespoon peppermint (or 2 peppermint tea bags)

8 almonds, crushed

¼ teaspoon mace

Heat the water on the stove and add the first three ingredients (following the "Process of Empowerment" on page 8), charging the potion with the desire to enhance and reveal the best qualities of Aquarius. After the potion has steeped, strain through a sieve and drink as desired.

This potion can be drunk whenever an extra boost of strength and energy is needed for those born under the sign of Aquarius, and it can also be used by anyone of any sign to aid in boosting mental abilities, creative insights, and community understanding.

Pisces
(February 19 to March 20)

This sign shifts the energy of wintertime, readying the environment for the cycle to begin again with the coming of spring. As the last sign of the zodiac, Pisces is considered to be the most mature. Those born under this sign usually have a somewhat dreamy nature and can be quite spiritual but should avoid the tendency to be too focused on fantasy or dreams to the exclusion of reality.

Keywords: Dreams, spirituality, secrets, hidden, unknown

★ Pisces Power Potion ★

Items Needed

2 cups water

1 tablespoon anise seeds

1 tablespoon catnip

1 teaspoon lemon juice

1 teaspoon lime juice

1 pinch cloves

Heat the water on the stove and add the next four ingredients (following the "Process of Empowerment" on page 8), charging the potion with the desire to enhance and reveal the best qualities of Pisces. While the potion is cooling, add the pinch of cloves. After the potion has steeped, strain through a sieve and drink as desired.

This potion can be drunk whenever an extra boost of strength and energy is needed for those born under the sign of Pisces, and it can be used by anyone of any sign to aid in increased spirituality, imagination, fantasy, artistic pursuits, and all forms of creativity.

The following small ritual is presented as an example for using the zodiac potions and is meant as one possibility, but not the only way.

★ Zodiac Chalice of Potential ★

Items Needed

1 candle (and holder)

Ingredients for the chosen zodiac recipe

Chalice

Cauldron (or other potion-making pot)

The color of the candle used should relate to the astrological sign of the potion being brewed. See Appendix 1: Magical Color Correspondences (on page 237) for the appropriate color correspondences or follow your intuition if you feel strongly pulled to a specific color. The candle can be charged with the intention that it will radiate the power of the specific zodiac sign (for example, gold or yellow for the power of Leo) by holding it in your hands and envisioning a glowing aura surrounding the candle in its same color. Once the candle has been charged, place it in the holder and set it in a safe place on the counter close to where you will prepare the potion. Light the candle.

The ingredients can be charged as stated in the recipes with the intention that the potion will "enhance and reveal the best qualities of (the chosen sign)"; each can be stirred into the water in the cauldron one at a time following the recipe's specific directions. After the potion has been prepared and cooled to the desired level, ladle some into the chalice, sweeten as needed, and hold the cup in both hands. Focus on the specific magical goal for which you have made this potion and mentally infuse that energy and desire into the liquid. A verbal spell can be created and spoken over the cup to further focus the magic. What follows is a simple rhyme:

> *Potion of power*
> *this Witch has made*
> *to reach my goal with stellar aid;*
> *wheel of stars, fill my cup with energy—*
> *I unleash this magic, so mote it be!*

After the spell has been spoken, drink the potion, taking into yourself the power you have raised. After this, snuff out the candle to end the rite.

Planetary Potion Recipes

This collection of potions draws upon the power of the primary planets and other celestial bodies that are most important in the field of astrology. The planets are said to be strongest when in direct motion and weak or troublesome when in retrograde motion. Though a bit of an optical illusion, a retrograde is when a planet is observed to be moving backward in its path from our vantage point through the zodiac. This phenomenon occurs when earth passes another planet in its orbit thus making it appear to us as though the other planet is moving backward. Though these potions can be used by people of any zodiac sign, they will be especially powerful for those born in the sign(s) the planet rules.

A word on the concept of ruling planets is in order. In astrology's ancient past, not all of the planets of which we are currently aware had been discovered. When designations were given as to which planets held the greatest influence over which signs, the farthest known planet in our solar system was Saturn. The planets Uranus, Neptune, and Pluto were not yet discovered, so the signs of Aquarius, Pisces, and Scorpio were originally assigned different planets as their rulers doubled up with other signs: Saturn for Aquarius, Jupiter for Pisces, and Mars for Scorpio. Today, we consider these planets the aforementioned signs' "classical rulers" and the outer planets their "modern rulers"— Uranus for Aquarius, Neptune for Pisces, and Pluto for Scorpio. Note as well that there are planets that even within the modern rule system still rule over more than one sign: Gemini and Virgo are both ruled by Mercury, and Taurus and Libra are both ruled by Venus. With the incorporation of the outer planets into modern astrology, my opinion is that we have a much clearer picture of those signs' energy. Though the modern rulers are now generally considered the main influence of those signs (that is, they best express their signs' energies), the classical planetary designations remain as the signs' "co-ruler" and are still considered to have some influence. I've dubbed the planet most often considered to be the dominant ruler of each sign as its "natural ruler" in this chapter to denote which energy is the most prominent for each zodiac sign. It is interesting to ponder whether or not in the future, as more discoveries and understandings are made about our solar system, if the other zodiac signs currently sharing a ruling planet will end up with differing assignments.

Another thing to note is that in the charging of these potions, I use the word "correct" to describe the type of energy being called upon. This word is deliberately neutral—depending upon the specific magical goal being worked for, the terms "positive" or "negative" or even "beneficial" may not exactly apply. Additionally, using this terminology helps ensure that disharmonious (that is, incorrect) energy is not called upon to charge the potions. Feel free to alter the phrasing if desired.

Sun

The center of this solar system and the star that makes possible our life on Earth, the sun has a potent energy aligned with creation, power, the self, and life. The sun is the natural ruler of Leo.

Keywords: Success, authority, fame, power

★ Sun Power Potion* ★

Items Needed

1 cup water

1 tablespoon black tea (or two tea bags)

1 teaspoon chicory

½ cup orange juice

½ cup pineapple juice

Heat the water and add the tea and chicory (following the "Process of Empowerment" on page 8), charging the potion with the desire that all the correct qualities of the sun are drawn into this potion. After the potion has steeped, strain through a sieve and mix with the orange and pineapple juices, then drink as desired.

This potion can be drunk whenever an extra boost of strength and energy is needed for magic related to success, good health, victory, wealth magic, and authority.

☿

Mercury

The planet with the swiftest orbit around the Sun, named after the Roman deity of commerce, communication, divination, travel, trickery, and luck, this planet shares a similar dominion. Though Mercury carries an unfortunate reputation as a troublemaker due to its frequent periods of retrograde, its energy can actually be extremely useful for sending and receiving messages, healing, and seeking knowledge. Mercury is the natural ruler of both Gemini and Virgo.

Keywords: Learning, writing, the mind, communication

★ Mercury Power Potion* ★

Items Needed

2 cups water

1 tablespoon lemongrass

1 tablespoon marjoram

5 hazelnuts, shelled and crushed

1 celery stalk, chopped

Heat the water on the stove and add the remaining ingredients (following the "Process of Empowerment" on page 8), charging the potion with the desire that all of the correct qualities of the planet Mercury are drawn into this potion.

After the potion has steeped, strain through a sieve and drink as desired.

This potion can be drunk whenever an extra boost of strength and energy is needed for magic related to communication, learning, healing, transportation and travel, and knowledge.

Venus

Known as the planet of love and relationships, Venus also has influence over contracts, marriage, and partnerships of all kinds whether personal or professional. Venus is the natural ruler of both Taurus and Libra.

Keywords: Love, friendship, partnership, marriage

★ Venus Power Potion* ★

Items Needed

1 cup water

¼ teaspoon cardamom

1 tablespoon spearmint

1 apricot, pitted and halved

1 tablespoon thyme

1 teaspoon raspberry jam

1 cup apple juice

Heat the water on the stove and add the next four ingredients (following the "Process of Empowerment" on page 8), charging the potion with the desire that all the correct qualities of the planet Venus are drawn into this potion. After the potion has steeped, strain through a sieve, stir in the raspberry jam and apple juice, and drink as desired.

This potion can be drunk whenever an extra boost of strength and energy is needed for magic related to love, friendship, emotional healing, beauty, and fertility.

☽
Moon

Though not specifically a planet, the power of the moon over life on Earth is well known. The moon has great influence over our oceans' tides. Spiritually, the moon speaks to our subconscious mind and magical side, granting us access into the psychic realm and aiding our abilities of divination, meditation, spellcasting, and connecting to goddess energy. The moon is the natural ruler of Cancer.

Keywords: Dreams, divination, psychic ability, the subconscious mind, goddess energy

★ Moon Power Potion* ★

Items Needed

    1 cup water

    1 tablespoon coconut flakes

1 peach, halved and pitted

1 pear, halved

2 tablespoons sugar (or substitute)

1 cup white wine or grape juice

Heat the water on the stove and add the remaining ingredients, placing the fruit cut sides down (following the "Process of Empowerment" on page 8), charging the potion with the desire that all of the correct qualities of the moon are drawn into this potion. After the potion has steeped, strain through a sieve, and drink as desired. The fruit can be eaten as well.

This potion can be drunk whenever an extra boost of strength and energy is needed for magic related to psychic ability, dreams, intuition, astral projection, and goddess energy.

Mars

Named after the Roman deity of war, this planet is charged with the energy of action. When a boost of power is needed, Mars can be of great assistance. When danger threatens or a stand needs to be made, this is a power to channel for success or victory. Mars is the natural ruler of Aries and the classical ruler of Scorpio (its modern co-ruler).

Keywords: Passion, force, aggression, courage, battle

★ Mars Power Potion* ★

Items Needed

    2 cups water

    1 tablespoon peppermint (or 2 peppermint tea bags)

    1 teaspoon basil

    1 teaspoon coriander

    ¼ teaspoon allspice

Heat the water on the stove and add the remaining ingredients (following the "Process of Empowerment" on page 8), charging the potion with the desire that all the correct qualities of the planet Mars are drawn into this potion. After the potion has steeped, strain through a sieve and drink as desired.

This potion can be drunk whenever an extra boost of strength and energy is needed for magic related to action, conflict, passion, sex, courage, determination and drive, and war.

♃

Jupiter

The largest planet in our solar system, Jupiter is known as a powerful embodiment of expansion, prosperity, and luck. This is the energy needed when seeking improvements, growth, and success. Jupiter is the natural ruler of Sagittarius and the classical ruler of Pisces (its modern co-ruler).

Keywords: Abundance, expansion, growth, prosperity, luck

★ Jupiter Power Potion* ★

Items Needed

> 2 cups water
>
> 1 tablespoon anise
>
> 1 tablespoon sage
>
> 2 figs, chopped
>
> ¼ teaspoon nutmeg

Heat the water on the stove and add the remaining ingredients (following the "Process of Empowerment" on page 8), charging the potion with the desire that all the correct qualities of the planet Jupiter are drawn into this potion. After the potion has steeped, strain through a sieve and drink as desired.

This potion can be drunk whenever an extra boost of strength and energy is needed for magic related to expansion and growth, luck, influence of those in power, wealth and success, legal matters, justice, and higher learning.

♄

Saturn

Despite its reputation as a harsh taskmaster, Saturn energy can offer critical assistance in matters such as hex-breaking, binding, and increasing self-discipline. Saturn is the natural ruler of Capricorn and the classical ruler of Aquarius as well (its modern co-ruler).

Keywords: Time, discipline, binding, hex making and breaking

★ Saturn Power Potion ★

Items Needed

    1 cup water

    1 teaspoon grapefruit zest

    1 plum, pitted and halved

    1 teaspoon mullein

    1 cup black cherry juice

Heat the water on the stove and add the next three ingredients (following the "Process of Empowerment" on page 8), charging the potion with the desire that all the correct qualities of the planet Saturn are drawn into this potion. After the potion has steeped, strain through a sieve and add the black cherry juice. Drink as desired.

This potion can be drunk whenever an extra boost of strength and energy is needed for magic related to time, binding, organization, restriction, neutralization, concentration, and discipline.

Uranus

Unpredictable and ever-changing, the energy of Uranus (sometimes spelled Ouranos) can be channeled for the developing of new and unusual ideas, art, scientific discoveries, and innovations into a workable form. If a block of inspiration is felt, the power of this planet can help remove the block. Uranus is the natural ruler of Aquarius.

Keywords: Electricity, genius, madness, spontaneity, community

★ Uranus Power Potion* ★

Items Needed

2 cups water

1 teaspoon peppermint (or 1 peppermint tea bag)

1 star anise, whole

3 tablespoons ground coffee

Sweetener (sugar, Stevia, or honey), to taste

Heat the water on the stove and add the next two ingredients (following the "Process of Empowerment" on page 8), remove from heat and add the coffee, charging the potion with the desire that all the correct qualities of the planet Uranus are drawn into this potion. After the potion has steeped, strain through a sieve and add sweetener if needed. Drink as desired.

This potion can be drunk whenever an extra boost of strength and energy is needed for magic related to invention, surprise, innovation, genius, spontaneity, restructuring, and electricity.

♆

Neptune

This planet, named in honor of a Roman deity of the sea, offers an energy that is attuned to dream-work, illusion, mysticism, scrying, creativity, emotional healing, nurturing, and all things spiritual. Neptune is the natural ruler of Pisces.

Keywords: Mysticism, dreams, spirituality, self-sacrifice, compassion

★ Neptune Power Potion ★

Items Needed

2 cups water

2 teaspoons mugwort

½ teaspoon poppy seeds

Sweetener (sugar, Stevia, or honey), to taste

Heat the water on the stove and add the mugwort and poppy seeds (following the "Process of Empowerment" on page 8), charging the potion with the desire that all the correct qualities of the planet Neptune are drawn into this potion. After the potion has steeped, strain through a sieve and add sweetener if needed (mugwort can be bitter). Drink as desired.

This potion can be drunk whenever an extra boost of strength and energy is needed for magic related to psychic ability, dreams, fantasy, artistic pursuits, imagination, healing, drugs and medications, and illusions.

♇

Pluto

Even though its planetary status may be subject to change, Pluto will always have astrological significance that matches and sometimes exceeds that of its fellow celestial bodies. The power of Pluto is limitless potential—an unrelenting drive to reach beyond any confines and explore the unknown. Although Pluto can offer the power to succeed against all odds, its energy should be used with caution: it can be harsh in its single-minded drive to victory. With its characteristic unstoppable force and ability to transform, it is the natural ruler of Scorpio.

Keywords: Transformation, breaking limits, power, force, rebirth

★ Pluto Power Potion ★

Items Needed

> 2 cups water
>
> 2 teaspoons wormwood
>
> 2 tablespoons wild mint (or 4 peppermint tea bags)
>
> Sweetener (sugar, Stevia, or honey), to taste

Heat the water on the stove and add the wormwood and mint (following the "Process of Empowerment" on page 8), charging the potion with the desire that all the correct qualities of the planet Pluto are drawn into this potion. After the potion has steeped, strain through a sieve and add sweetener if needed (wormwood can be bitter). Drink as desired.

This potion can be drunk whenever an extra boost of strength and energy is needed for magic related to transformation, transcending limitations, seemingly impossible manifestations, to bring order or to bring chaos, death, and the unknown.

))●((

Though simply drinking a potion while focusing on an intention helps to empower your magic toward manifesting that goal, more formal methods can be employed to focus the magic. The following spell is one way to utilize a planetary potion in magic. This spell calls upon the energy of the chosen planet to help manifest your magical goal.

★ Planetary Power Candle Spell ★

Items Needed

1 candle (and holder)

Athame or carving tool

Ingredients for chosen planetary recipe

Chalice

Cauldron (or other potion-making pot)

The color of the candle used should relate to the planet of the potion being brewed. See appendix 1 (on page 237) for the planetary color alignments (e.g., red for the power of Mars). The candle can be charged with the intention that it will channel and radiate the power of the specific planet by holding it in your hands and envisioning a glowing aura surrounding the candle in its same color. Using the athame or carving tool, etch the glyph (symbol) of the planet whose energy you are trying to call upon onto the candle. While focusing on your specific magical goal, lightly anoint the candle with some of your saliva from the candle's wick to the base. Once the candle has been charged, place it in the holder, set it in a safe place on the counter close to where you are going to prepare the potion, and light it.

The ingredients can be charged as stated in the recipes with the intention that all the correct qualities of (the chosen planet) are drawn into this potion and can each be stirred into the water in the cauldron one at a time following any specific directions in the recipe. After the potion has been prepared and cooled to the desired level, ladle some into the chalice (sweetening as needed) and hold the cup in both hands. Focus again on the specific magical goal for which you have made this potion and mentally infuse that energy and intention into the liquid. A verbal spell can be created and spoken over the cup to add to the magic's focus. The following rhyme is an example:

> *Planet (name of planet), your power I seek,*
> *to reach my goal and achieve my aim;*
> *with this magical potion I drink,*
> *influence absorbed and energy claimed!*

After the spell has been spoken, drink the potion, taking the power you have raised into yourself. The candle can be left to burn afterward for as long as is safe and then snuffed out. The spell is complete.

(((●)))

All of the astrological potions found in this chapter have
been designed to fortify and empower; enhancing our
inherent abilities and helping us to gain new strengths. I
have always believed that using potions of this type is a
wonderful means of bringing magic within and keeping our
personal energies vibrant and attuned to our most beneficial
qualities. Not all potions are crafted as enhancements, however—some are made to remove or neutralize unwanted
energies. In that spirit, the following chapter explores several options for purification and cleansing potions as well as
banishing recipes utilizing a variety of ingredients and pro-
cedures for making these powerful concoctions.

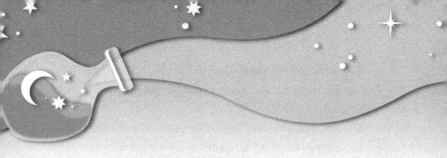

Chapter 4
CLEANSING AND
BANISHING RECIPES

Spiritual cleansing, purification, exorcism, and banishing are all related but differing magical practices which center on the concept that harmful or incompatible forces and energies can be neutralized, transformed, or removed through the power of an energetic and focused act of magical intention, emotion, and willpower. At first glance, use of the words "cleansing" and "purification" could imply that some form of impurity or uncleanliness might be present, but that is simply a limit of language. It would be more accurate to say that disharmonious or incorrect energy is brought back into alignment or balance. Working within this understanding, there are many, many methods of magical cleansing; everything from simple affirmation and prayer to full-scale intensive group ritual. Keeping within the scope of this book, this chapter presents several potion recipes for magical cleansing and realignment as well as mixtures for banishing and rebalancing energy.

Where cleansing and purification are mostly centered on rebalancing energy or neutralizing harm, banishing is more focused on removing and casting away that which is either specifically harmful or simply just that which is no longer in harmony with our current needs or desires. Cleansing and purification are kind of like washing a dish to return it to a good and useful condition whereas banishing is like throwing the dish in the garbage to be rid of it forever. Both types of intention are addressed in this chapter, but let's begin with cleansing.

★ Gentle Cleansing Potion* ★

This delicate mixture helps restore balance and energetic harmony through the properties of the herbs and other ingredients. It is a good potion to use to help relieve the persistent astral residue of things such as work stress or the chaos of being in large crowds for an extended length of time.

Items Needed

1 cup water

1 tablespoon peppermint

1 tablespoon thyme

2 teaspoons rosemary

½ cup lemon juice

Sweetener (sugar, Stevia, or honey), to taste

Sugar has cleansing properties and as referenced in *Cunningham's Encyclopedia of Magical Herbs* (Llewellyn, 2006), has been used in Hawaiian magic to dispel evil or scattered to cleanse an area before ritual. Stevia and honey both have healing qualities, so any of these options would be appropriate. Heat the water on the stove and add the herbs (following the "Process of Empowerment" on page 8) and the lemon juice, charging the potion with the desire that it shall cleanse and balance anyone who drinks it. After the potion has steeped, strain through a sieve and add sweetener if using. Drink as desired.

If a stronger cleansing is required (for example, due to being around too many negative people, upsetting events, intense arguments, or suspected psychic attack), the next potion can be very useful.

★ Extra-Strength Cleansing Potion ★

You can sweeten this a bit if desired but it is definitely not the best-tasting potion in the world. A better method of ingestion is stirring it into a spaghetti sauce and serving it over pasta for a meal. Either way, its cleansing power will be absorbed.

Items Needed

2 cups water

½ teaspoon turmeric

⅛ teaspoon cayenne pepper

¼ teaspoon onion powder

¼ teaspoon garlic powder

2 tablespoons basil

1 tablespoon nettle

Charge the ingredients and brew in the usual manner. If using the pasta sauce method, this potion does not really need to be strained since the herbs (even the nettle) should complement the flavor already present in the sauce. As the potion is stirred into the sauce, the whole mixture can be charged with the intention that the sauce and potion shall cleanse and balance all who eat it.

)((●))

A pleasant means of using a potion for cleansing is to make and drink a cordial specifically designed to provide that inner energetic rebalancing.

★ Cleansing Cordial ★

This recipe yields a sweet, strong, purifying alcoholic beverage that can be used to aid purification and balancing of the energy. It takes two months to create but is worth the effort.

Items Needed

> 1 cup sugar
>
> ½ cup lavender
>
> 2 cups blueberries
>
> 2 cups blackberries
>
> 4 cups vodka

Charge each of the ingredients separately before making the cordial. When ready, add the sugar to a large container with an airtight lid. Top with the lavender and berries, and add the vodka last. Let the container steep for two months in a cool, dark place away from sunlight, being sure to gently shake it once or twice per week. Once the two months have passed, carefully strain the liquid and decant into a new bottle. To use, either drink ¼ cup of this potion on its own or mix it with a cup of your favorite lemonade—lemons are purifying in nature as well.

The Magical Shrub

A shrub (in this case, not a decorative plant) is a sweetened fruit (and sometimes herbal) vinegar-based drink or drink addition. This drink is said to have been invented centuries ago, when people preserved fresh fruits in sugar to draw out the fruit liquid that would then ferment into vinegar. In modern times, shrubs are seeing a bit of a revival as cocktail mixers. The modern versions are quite easy to make—all you have to do is add vinegar to the product instead of waiting for fermentation. Though this is not specifically a potion, in my sense of the term at least, shrubs can be used as a key ingredient in the making of a potion.

Among the magical properties of sugar are cleansing and purification and certain types of fruit share this quality as does the vinegar. Though primarily associated with love, peaches have also been used for healing, for cleansing, and to drive off evil. Ginger is a natural aid to digestion and has power-boosting abilities, and cinnamon is a spiritual spice with healing properties. Combined, they make a delightfully sweet and spicy concoction that blends very well with the rest of the potion to make a complete formula for magical cleansing.

★ Peach Spice Shrub* ★

Items Needed

½ teaspoon cinnamon

2 teaspoons sliced fresh ginger

1 cup sliced peaches

1 cup sugar

1 cup vinegar (white wine or champagne vinegar work best)

Empower each of the ingredients for cleansing. Combine the cinnamon, ginger, peaches, and sugar in a bowl with a sturdy lid, mashing a bit to blend. Allow the mixture to sit covered for at least an hour, then add the vinegar. Re-cover and refrigerate for at least two days. When ready, pour the shrub through a sieve into a clean jar. Discard the solids and the shrub is ready. Keep it in the refrigerator.

★ Shrub Purifying Potion ★

Items Needed

1 tablespoon peppermint

1 tablespoon lavender

1 cup water

¼ cup peach spice shrub

1 cup club soda, chilled

Empower the herbs with purifying intention and combine them with the water. Brew in a cauldron in the usual manner then remove from heat and allow the liquid to cool completely. Once cooled, strain into a glass, stir in the shrub, and finally, slowly add the club soda. Drink and allow the potion to cleanse and purify.

((●))

Cleansing and purification are important practices that can bring us back into inner balance and harmony where we otherwise may have been left to flounder in the chaos or static of incompatible or harmful energies. Not only helpful for keeping a sense of calm in everyday life, these practices can be crucial in the working of other forms of magic, as they neutralize energy that could be incompatible with or even oppose your magical goal. If, however, the problem is more stubborn in nature, it might be necessary for actual banishing. These next recipes will focus on this.

Banishing

Banishing is sometimes viewed in harsh terms. I've seen it equated to hexing and sometimes it is even seen as dark magic with anger-filled energies being thrown at innocent victims to cast them away in a dramatic and permanent fashion. While this *could* be an act of banishing, the types most often practiced are far more practical and much less harsh. The type described here is first and foremost focused on realigning the energies in an area, within an object, person, or animal in order to create the correct balance of forces to restore harmony. Banishing is not exclusively about sending someone away, but also about transformation, renewal, alignment, harmony, and balance within the self or environment.

Though the cleansing potions provide a helpful means of rebalancing our energy and can help us recover from feeling overwhelmed by the energy of others, sometimes stronger magic is required to rid ourselves of more serious issues such as the rare but nevertheless legitimate concern of psychic attack. In such cases where a hex, curse, or psychic attack is known to have been made, a good, strong potion like the following recipe can be used to banish the harmful magic.

★ Hex-Breaking Potion ★

If a psychic attack is not only suspected but confirmed (such as if someone has made a direct threat), then drink one cup of this potion every night for seven nights during a waning moon to help neutralize any harmful power sent your way.

Items Needed

2 cups water

2 tablespoons nettle

1 tablespoon elder flowers

1 teaspoon basil

2 cups blueberries (or huckleberries)

Sweetener (sugar, Stevia, or honey), to taste

Charge each ingredient with the intention that the potion will dissolve any harmful energy in your system, and fill each ingredient with as much universal white light as you can envision. Brew the herbs in the water in the usual way. After it has cooled, muddle the berries into the potion, and then strain it and drink as needed, sweetening if preferred. If you would like to further clarify your magical intention, chant a spell or charm such as the one that follows before drinking this potion:

> *Harmful magic, your power now broken,*
> *the hex is banished and blessed I'll be;*
> *filled with the power from this potion,*
> *renewed and restored, unbound and free.*

Drink the potion to absorb its power and break the hex.

The range of options in regard to banishing brews and how to use them are quite varied, which is helpful since the more magical options we have at our disposal, the greater chance we have of finding one that perfectly suits our individual needs and purposes.

★ Boundary Ward Banishing Brew ★

This first brew addresses banishing as a method of warding away evil and harm. I used this recipe in my example in the "Process of Empowerment" (on page 8) and the chant(s) given there can be used when making this brew. The nettles are added because they are a powerful banisher of harmful forces. The mullein is added to ward away harmful animals and creatures, and the onion is an excellent ward against malevolent spiritual forces.

Items Needed

  2 cups water

  1 tablespoon nettle

  1 tablespoon mullein

  1 tablespoon chopped onion

Charge each of the ingredients, then add to the water and simmer in a pot (following the "Process of Empowerment" on page 8), charging the brew with the desire that it "shall halt and repel all harmful energies, people, creatures, or forces." Remove from heat. Once cooled, strain the brew into a cup and use it to encircle the exterior of your home or property. It can also be used to recharge other wards such as amulets placed around your home by anointing them with the brew, provided they are able to withstand moisture.

((●))

If a simpler energetic shift is all that is required, a light banishing brew can be created that acts as a sort of magical lens or prism through which incompatible energies pass and are realigned into a beneficial form. The easiest method for this is to create a decorative bottle that can be placed in the area needing the change. This will basically be a form of witch bottle.

★ Banishing Bad Energy Brew ★

To help preserve this brew after it is placed in its bottle, ¼ teaspoon of bleach or tincture of benzoin can be added in to prevent the herb particles from molding.

Items Needed

    2 cups water

    2 teaspoons basil

    1 teaspoon sage

    1 teaspoon tarragon

    1 teaspoon rosemary

    1 teaspoon thyme

    1 teaspoon lavender

    1 teaspoon catnip

Empower the herbs with white light energy to transform bad to good, harmful to beneficial, and brew in the usual manner. No need to strain this one, if the herbs remain within, it helps the magic work more efficiently. Once the brew has cooled, pour it into a clear, pink, or light blue glass bottle with an airtight lid. Once the lid is sealed, place the bottle in a prominent place wherever the change is needed, making as many as necessary if multiple rooms need this magic.

$((●))$

If a strong removal of harmful or incompatible forces is needed, call upon the four elements of fire, air, water, and earth to banish and cleanse the area and then fill that energy vacuum with peace, blessings, and protection from further problems.

★ Elemental Banishing Brew* ★

Though this brew is aligned with the four elements, its strongest component is elemental fire's banishing power; this influence is then balanced by the addition of the other three elements to add beneficial qualities so that the energetic vacuum created from the banishing is properly filled.

Items Needed

2 cups water

1 teaspoons cinnamon, for fire and success

1 teaspoons black pepper, for fire and banishing

1 teaspoon rosemary, for fire and banishing

1 teaspoon garlic powder, for fire and banishing

1 teaspoon sage, for air and cleansing

2 chamomile tea bags, for water and peace

1 teaspoon salt, for earth, blessing, and protection

Empower each ingredient for the intention given and brew in the usual way. After the brew has cooled and been strained, it can be sprinkled in the corners of each room or poured into a bowl in which a heavy white or black candle has been placed. With the bowl set on a sturdy surface, light the candle. When the candle sputters into the brew and goes out, the room will be cleared. This can be done in each room for a full house banishing. Since this brew contains salt, do not use it outdoors on the land. It can be used to sprinkle under the mat at the front door to halt those who wish to cause harm.

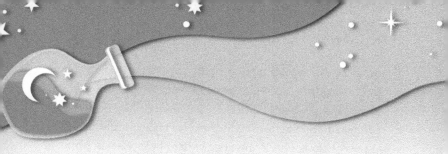

Chapter 5
HEALING POTIONS
AND ELIXIRS

Of all the amazing magical pursuits available to try, perhaps the most transformative is healing. To move oneself (or especially another) from illness and imbalance back to a state of good health is so powerful and deeply emotionally satisfying that I believe it is one of the most noble of magical practices. In legend, the Witch always had a mysterious role to play, and those who sought her aid for healing were usually in dire need. It is from this notion that we continue to draw a sense of mystique as modern Witches who work healing magic. Even in our modern age, many people still seek the aid of Witches and other mystical people for assistance and healing. Though many today enjoy the benefits of modern medicine, there is still a great number of "alternative" healing techniques we can use to boost our strength, maintain good health, or restore our inner balance. A favorite healing method of mine is the use of tonics, elixirs, and potions. This magic is wonderfully effective, has a "mediciney" vibe to it, and is not as energetically taxing as heavy ritual—a plus if you are trying to heal yourself from an illness.

Incidentally, the use of any type of healing magic on others tends to bring up discussions of magical ethics. If anything, potion making only adds to the list of ethical considerations and potential pitfalls. While there are many that firmly believe that permission should always be obtained from someone before doing any type of magic on them in order to avoid any issues of manipulation or possible harm, there is another school of thought. If you build into the intention of any magic that it is being performed according to the subject's free will, then any spell directed at someone will only work if they allow it on an unconscious level. This helps to avoid any breach of magical ethics though some may still take objection to this, but that is something which must be decided by each practitioner on their own. With potion magic, my personal opinion is that it is best to inform anyone of the nature of the potion before they drink it, not only for the ethical concerns of giving something to ingest to a person without their knowledge or consent, but also to avoid any potential allergic reactions to any ingredients. For those who have them, food allergies are a serious concern and should not be taken lightly.

One of my most important life lessons was about the importance of what we eat and drink and its effect upon health. According to the World Health Organization, "cardiovascular diseases, the major killers worldwide, are to a great extent due to unbalanced diets and physical inactivity."[2] The WHO/FAO Expert Consultation on Diet, Nutrition, and the Prevention of Chronic Diseases met in Geneva in January of 2002 to examine the science base of the relationship between diet and physical activity patterns and the major nutrition-related chronic diseases. According to their findings, reducing the amounts of high fat foods as well as those high in sugar and salt can be some of the most crucial steps in the prevention of most of the major chronic diseases found in the world. It has been estimated that 85 percent of disease can be directly attributed to lifestyle, and a large part of our lifestyles is what we take into our bodies. What does this have to do with magic? Well, aside from the fact that a chapter on any type of healing (magical or not) would be incomplete without addressing what has been found to be the major cause of chronic illness, the ingredients of potions, tonics, and elixirs are edible and therefore food. If we acknowledge

2. Diet, Nutrition, and the Prevention of Chronic Diseases. Report of the joint WHO/FAO expert consultation. https://www.who.int /dietphysicalactivity/publications/trs916/summary/en/.

the power of any food-based ingredients such as herbs when it comes to healing, why wouldn't we recognize the critical impact any foods can have upon our overall health? Though it may seem like a diversion to discuss food and the World Health Organization, a complete picture of health is, in my opinion, an important facet of any type of healing work.

Before proceeding, here are two cautions regarding the recipes featuring alcohol in this chapter: they should not be given to children and they should not be used shortly before driving or operating any heavy equipment. Now with that heavy discussion out of the way, let us return to the topic at hand—recipes for magical healing potions. These first two potions were featured in my 2013 book, *Supermarket Magic* (Llewellyn), and relate to healing and improving the condition of an upset stomach.

★ (Overall) Healing Potion* ★

This potion is both cleansing and healing in its nature, can provide relief for headache pain, stomach troubles, and cold symptoms and help bring the body back into balance.

Items Needed

  2 cups water

  2 tablespoons rosemary

  2 tablespoons spearmint

  1 teaspoon sage

1 teaspoon thyme

Juice of ½ lemon

1 tablespoon honey

Charge the herbs with healing intent and then brew them in the water and strain into a cup. Add the lemon juice and honey, stirring to mix. Sip the potion slowly allowing its energy to spread through your body, going to points in need of healing.

★ Stomach Tonic* ★

This potion is specifically designed to soothe an upset stomach whether from illness or questionable food. Though the mint does have soothing properties, its inclusion here is primarily to impart a more pleasant flavor and if desired, it can be left out without spoiling the potion's effectiveness, because mint can sometimes be too much for a delicate system.

Items Needed

2 cups water

1 teaspoon marjoram (or oregano)

1 teaspoon thyme

1 teaspoon sage

1 tablespoon peppermint

Brew this in the usual manner and strain into a mug. Sweeten if desired and sip the tonic slowly to help calm the digestive system.

((●))

If stomach troubles lead to what I will call "intestinal issues," the following potion can prove to be a great help. There really is no adequate way to tactfully name this potion so I might as well be direct.

★ Anti-Diarrhea Tonic ★

Items Needed

2 cups water

2 tablespoons mullein

2 tablespoons catnip

Sweetener (sugar, Stevia, or honey), to taste

Simmer the herbs in the water for fifteen minutes and then strain into a large mug. Drink as warm as you can, lightly sweetened if desired. A second serving of this can be brewed and drunk if needed.

★ Anti-Pain Potion ★

Here is a simple potion to help ease inflammation and mild to moderate pain.

Items Needed

> 2 cups water
>
> 1 tablespoon white willow bark
>
> 1 tablespoon nettle
>
> 1 teaspoon cramp bark
>
> 1 tablespoon hyssop (herb only—do not use the essential oil)
>
> 1 tablespoon orange peel

Empower the herbs with soothing ice blue light energy to help stop pain. Boil the willow bark in the water for fifteen minutes then remove from heat, add the remaining herbs, cover, and let steep for another ten minutes. Strain and drink a cup of the potion warm. Repeat with another cup if necessary.

★ Flu-Battle Potion ★

This concoction is a powerful and vitalizing tonic that can help strengthen the body in its fight against colds and flu symptoms. It is filled with soothing and healing ingredients, and many of the herbs are rich in minerals and other helpful nutrients. Since there are so many herbs and things in this recipe, it is a good idea to create a large batch of the dry ingredients in a jar at the beginning of the cold part of the year so that you can simply take a couple spoonfuls and make a convenient cup or two of the potion anytime it might be needed. Each of the dry ingredient amounts can be quadrupled for the large batch and stored in a canning jar, then when needed two tablespoons of the mixed dried ingredients can be added to each cup of water used. For a single-cup serving, the lemon juice and honey amounts can be adjusted to a half teaspoon each or to taste.

Items Needed

6 cups water

1 tablespoon thyme

1 tablespoon sage

1 tablespoon fennel seeds

1 tablespoon nettle leaves

1 tablespoon crushed rose hips

1 tablespoon elder flowers

1 tablespoon elder berries, crushed

1 tablespoon hyssop (herb only—do not use hyssop oil for this!)

¼ teaspoon ginger

½ teaspoon lemongrass

½ teaspoon licorice root

½ teaspoon grated orange peel

1 tablespoon lemon juice

1 tablespoon honey

Brew all of the herbs and spices together in the water in the usual way, then strain and add the lemon juice and honey. Serve hot and sip a cup or two slowly for relief. One word of caution regarding hyssop: it can be omitted entirely, if desired. Though as an herb it has been used in the kitchen for ages, high concentrations of its essential oils can cause seizures or convulsions in some people. For this reason, the essential oil should not be used in this potion. Additionally, anyone pregnant or nursing should not use hyssop. This potion really does help fortify the body and speed relief. I became very sick in November of 2019 and credit this very potion with not only helping me to recover from the flu but also helping me to avoid a recurrence two months later when everyone in the household got sick except me—and it helped them recover too.

(((●)))

A famous tonic created by respected author and herbalist Rosemary Gladstar to strengthen the immune system, aid digestion, and help fight colds and the flu is Fire Cider Tonic. Though it doesn't count as a potion per se, it is a solid herbal remedy that bears mentioning; my version most certainly does count as a potion and is a bit gentler for those who might not be a fan of the full-strength apple cider vinegar base of the classic tonic recipe.

★ Furie Cider Potion* ★

Everything in the mixture can be obtained from a supermarket though fresh horseradish and turmeric may be harder to find.

Items Needed

- 1 tablespoon rosemary
- ½ cup chopped onions
- 3 garlic cloves, crushed
- ¼ teaspoon cayenne pepper
- ¼ teaspoon chopped horseradish
- ½ teaspoon turmeric
- 1 cup water
- ½ cup honey
- 1 cup apple cider
- ½ cup apple cider vinegar

Charge each of the items with the intention of healing and add the first six ingredients with the water into a cauldron. Simmer covered on low heat until the water begins to boil (which should happen rather quickly due to the small amount of liquid). Remove from heat and allow it to completely cool while covered. Once cooled, pour the liquid (without straining) into a canning jar or any bottle with a tight-fitting lid. Next, stir in the honey, apple cider,

and vinegar. Allow the potion to steep on the counter overnight then strain into a clean bottle and refrigerate. When
in need, drink a quarter to half cup of the cider daily to
help ward off illness.

))●((

If coughing or lung complaints are more specifically the issue,
this next potion can be taken to help bring relief. It is filled
with herbs which not only have magical healing qualities but
have homeopathic and nutritionally vitalizing properties for
the lungs and throat as well.

★ Pulmonary Pick Me Up Potion ★

In addition to drinking this potion, as it is being brewed,
the rising steam can be carefully inhaled to help bring relief.

Items Needed

   3 cups water

   1 tablespoon mullein

   1 tablespoon sage

   1 tablespoon mint

   1 tablespoon oregano

   1 tablespoon thyme

   1 tablespoon licorice root

1 tablespoon slippery elm

½ teaspoon horehound (optional)

Charge the herbs for healing with special emphasis on being able to breathe clearly, free of coughs or congestion. Brew up in the usual way and allow it to cool slightly. Drink a cupful, making sure to take it as warm as you can. Sip as slowly to help relief. This potion can be drunk three times per day until relief is felt, if needed.

))●((

Another potion that is good to have in your magical pantry, not only for times of illness but also as a go-to soother, is a good sleeping potion, such as the following recipe.

★ Sleeping Potion ★

Where would a book of Witch's magical brews be without a sleeping potion? Despite the cliché of old-timey sleeping potions, their availability is exceedingly sparse. While there are many herbal teas and tonics that are said to aid in treating insomnia or helping to fall asleep, it is surprisingly difficult to find genuine nontoxic sleeping potion recipes. This version is nontoxic (unless you are allergic to an ingredient, of course) but should not be consumed by anyone pregnant or with severe health problems. It is pretty powerful; the first time I brewed and drank this potion, I slept for twelve hours straight, so make sure that you do not have to be up early the next day the first time you try this. An important note is warranted here: valerian smells horrible and has a rather odd taste but is a very strong sleep-inducing herb and should therefore not be omitted. Be sure to store valerian in an airtight container away from heat. Additionally, a lot of cats are really attracted to the smell of this herb, even ones that don't respond strongly to catnip. Valerian is best stored out of their reach as well.

Items Needed

- 1½ cups water
- 1 tablespoon valerian
- 1 tablespoon hops (can be substituted with a tablespoon of catnip or lavender)
- 1 tablespoon chamomile
- 2 teaspoons mugwort
- Sugar or sweetener, to taste

Charge each herb with a deep indigo-blue energy to align their energies with sleep. Simmer them in the water in the usual manner. After it has cooled a bit, strain one cupful into a mug and add the chosen sweetener to taste. I highly recommend adding sweetener—though this potion is very effective, it tastes rather foul. Feel free to increase the amount of chamomile for a (slightly) smoother taste.

Elixirs

When it comes to elixirs, there are three basic definitions of the word: (1) a cure-all; (2) a miraculous substance such as a potion to grant immortality; and (3) a sweetened solution of a medicine in alcohol and water. It is with these definitions in mind that the elixirs featured in this book were created, though for some is another word that also fits— "cocktail." I've personally always found it fun to explore the familiar and see things in new ways; discovering the magical and spiritual properties of items and recipes that people already use has always been a fascinating subject of study.

One of what we consider today a classic liquor that has been made for centuries began its life as a medicinal preparation—a healing potion, if you will—and due to its herbal content and strong properties, still possesses a powerful energy of transformation. That liquor is gin. What we know as gin is a distilled liquor that is enhanced with herbs, and the exact combination and potency of these herbs can change from one manufacturer to another. The only real requirement is that in order to be called gin, the distilled grain alcohol must contain juniper. Juniper is a very magically potent herb that contains the power to break hexes; increase psychic ability; grant protection from theft, spirits, wild animals, and accidents; and can also bolster good health and ward off illness. Vermouth is another alcoholic beverage that was originally taken as a heath tonic and is a fortified and lightly sweetened herbal wine mixture with varying proprietary recipes. Its primary magical properties are healing and fertility, and as a drink for lunar magic. Vermouth is featured as an important ingredient in the next two recipes. The first cocktail/elixir we will look at is a version of a classic drink that my partner and I have created and perfected over the years—what I like to call the "Furie-Witch Martini."

★ Furie-Witch Martini* ★

This cocktail is a strong, savory blend of a standard dirty martini (contains conventional martini ingredients along with added olive brine) and a Gibson, a classic martini with cocktail onions as garnish instead of the usual green olives or twist of citrus peel. I've added tablespoon conversions because even though cocktail recipes are often given in ounce measurements, I usually end up using my tablespoon. This recipe yields one martini.

Items Needed

Ice

2½ ounces gin (5 tablespoons or ⅓ cup)

½ ounce dry vermouth (1 tablespoon)

½ ounce olive brine (1 tablespoon)

½ ounce cocktail onion brine (1 tablespoon)

3 green olives and/or cocktail onions for garnish

Charge each of the ingredients with the magical intention (healing, cleansing, or both) and then pour the liquids into a cocktail shaker that has been filled with ice. Shake as desired and strain the mixture into a chilled martini glass adding the preferred garnishes. Sip slowly and feel the magic of the elixir taking effect.

★ Furie-Witch Martini Sparkler* ★

In this second version of our signature drink, there is only one added ingredient; club soda. Club soda is water, minerals, and bubbles and is thus linked to the element of water (of course) as well as the earth and the moon. It has the magical properties of releasing energy and uniting elements and can thus be used to increase the speed, potency, and effectiveness of magical potions and elixirs. Not only that, but for practical reasons it can also dilute stronger drinks if there is a desire to consume them over a longer period of time.

Items Needed

1 prepared recipe Furie-Witch Martini (two if you're feeling adventurous)

Ice

1 liter club soda, chilled

Garnishes (cocktail onions, green olives, or both)

Charge the club soda with intent while it is still in the bottle. In a medium-sized pitcher, add some ice and then combine the martini mixture and the club soda stirring lightly to blend. Pour the drinks into regular cocktail glasses adding an odd number of garnishes (it is considered bad luck to have an even number of olives) and enjoy.

《《●》》

This next elixir is an excellent one for those chilly autumn and winter nights; versions of it have been used for generations to help fight colds and flu.

★ Gin Hot Toddy* ★

Though most people think of whiskey when they think of hot toddies, a fine alternative can be made with gin. This is a wonderfully soothing drink when feeling under the weather and can be used not only as a healing elixir when sick but also as a general tonic during wintertime to help combat seasonal fatigue. If you'd prefer a classic hot toddy, 1½ ounces of whiskey can be substituted for the gin. The honey and lemon can be adjusted to taste, and a vegan sweetener can be used in place of the honey with similar success, if that is a concern.

Items Needed

6 ounces (¾ cup) water

1 tablespoon honey

1½ ounces gin

1 tablespoon lemon juice

1 lemon slice

1 cinnamon stick

Charge each of the ingredients for healing. Add only the water to a cauldron and bring it to a simmer. Remove from heat and pour the water into a mug. Add the honey to the water, stirring lightly to dissolve. Pour in the gin and add the lemon juice and slice and cinnamon stick. Sip slowly and feel the warmth and healing power being absorbed.

★ Tooth Be Numb* ★

I don't know that this qualifies specifically as an elixir, but it is an important inclusion. When tooth pain happens, it needs to be stopped as soon as possible.

Items Needed

¼ cup gin

½ teaspoon cloves, crushed

The method of preparation for this is pretty quick, which is a definite plus. Pour the gin into a bottle or jar with a tight-fitting lid. Add the cloves and shake or stir it to blend the mixture. After the cloves have settled to the bottom of the jar, strain the elixir.

To use, take a spoonful of this elixir and swish it around in your mouth, allowing it to cover the affected tooth. This mixture works quite well, but will at first cause a sharp pain in the problem tooth (warning: hurts like hell!) but then will deaden the nerve for some time afterward. This can be done as often as needed but remember not to drive directly after administering this particular remedy. Also, this remedy does not replace visiting a dentist; it will simply take away the unrelenting agony in the meantime. I assume that vodka could be used instead of the gin, but this is the recipe as I learned and used it.

★ Anti-Cough Elixir Syrup* ★

This final healing elixir is a classic, but one that should come with modern warnings. Since there is alcohol in it, this elixir should not be used by children, pregnant women, those with a drinking problem, or anyone who needs to operate a motor vehicle within the next few hours. That being said, this mixture is anti-microbial, a soothing expectorant, and helps to reduce sore throat pain.

Items Needed

2 tablespoons apple cider vinegar

2 tablespoons olive oil

8 tablespoons honey

1 tablespoon chopped fresh ginger

¼ teaspoon cayenne pepper

2 tablespoons whiskey

Combine all the ingredients into a jar and stir well to blend. Allow the elixir to sit overnight and then strain the mixture into another jar and refrigerate. Use 1 or 2 teaspoons at a time up to four times per day to help relieve coughs and sore throat.

(((●)))

These potion and elixir recipes are each soothing and healing in their own way, and I hope that they will bring the benefit of improved health to any who might be in need of their magic.

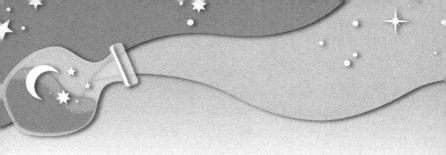

Chapter 6
LOVE, MONEY,
AND LUCK RECIPES

I was hesitant to include love potions in this chapter; what have historically been considered "love potions" are mostly a collection of manipulative and/or toxic formulations designed to overcome the will of another. Not only do such mixtures fall well outside my personal ethical boundaries, many of them are also viciously disturbing in their preparation—no boiled toads or stolen body parts will be needed here! Instead of the gruesome, what's presented here is a small collection of potions that can be used to enhance one's ability to magically attract love, romance, or even simply sexual encounters. There are also a couple of recipes to strengthen and encourage love already present between partners, and at the end you'll find formulas for gaining money and recipes for improving luck.

Love

Love, romance, and sex are such important parts of life for many people, and the magically minded are no exception. Love spells of all types are still the most popular of magical subjects (in addition to money magic), and love potions are a classic facet of this sort of magic. Hopefully, this look at their modern usage adds a practical element to the subject.

This first recipe is a simple but powerful drink designed to magically intensify the attractiveness of those who drink it. It grants a compelling magnetism to the user that will grab the attention of others without attempting to dominate their free will. This potion is meant to pique the interest of potential partners and can be used to seek potential love interests or more casual encounters, if preferred.

★ Magnetic Attraction Potion ★

Items Needed

½ teaspoon black pepper

½ teaspoon nettle seeds

½ cup water

1 (750 ml) bottle of red wine

Empower the herbs and crush them together. Simmer them in the water just until steam begins to rise then remove the cauldron from heat and allow the liquid to cool completely. Strain the cooled liquid and add it to the wine. This wine is now a potion that when shared, will help to reinforce an attraction between the people drinking it.

(((●))

The next potion has a dual purpose: not only does it serve to attract others, it also acts as a mild aphrodisiac on the user so that the proper mood is set for a night of passion and romance. A version of this recipe appears in the interesting and unusual book, *Witches' Potions and Spells* (Peter Pauper Press, 1971) by Kathryn Paulsen, but more recently a modern version has been featured in my book, *Supermarket Magic* (Llewellyn, 2013) as a love perfume recipe to attract men. This recipe is for a drinkable potion. There's something about this combination of spices and herbs that act as an aphrodisiac to men, so this potion should only be used by someone wishing to attract men specifically.

★ Sexy Spice Potion (Men Attracting) ★
Items Needed

2 cups water

1 tablespoon cinnamon

1 teaspoon nutmeg

1 teaspoon ginger

2 teaspoons allspice

½ teaspoon cloves

1 tablespoon lavender

Empower the spices and brew in the usual manner. Once the potion is cooled, strain, sweeten as desired, and drink to infuse yourself with attraction power.

★ Sexy Spice Potion (Woman Attracting) ★

Items Needed

2 cups water

1 tablespoon crushed rose petals

1 teaspoon catnip

1 teaspoon lavender

½ teaspoon pure vanilla extract

¼ teaspoon nutmeg

Empower the herbs and spices and brew in the usual manner. Strain the cooled potion and drink to be infused with the attraction power. This potion can be used by anyone wishing to attract women.

❨❨●❩❩

The following potion is a little complicated but can be used by everybody. It is made in two stages.

★ The Love Shrub* ★

The name of this one just doesn't sound right to me, but that's what it is—a potion made from a shrub, a sweetened vinegar-based drink. Though the earlier shrub recipe was focused on cleansing and purification, this one uses ingredients attuned to attracting love.

Items Needed

½ cup chopped apples

½ cup chopped apricots

½ cup lightly mashed cherries

1 cup sugar

1½ cups apple cider vinegar

Empower each ingredient with love. Combine the fruits in a bowl and cover with the sugar and stir to blend. Let the mixture sit covered for at least two hours to overnight, then add the apple cider vinegar. Re-cover and refrigerate for two days. Next, pour the shrub through a sieve into a clean jar with a lid. If the lid is metal, place some plastic wrap underneath it so that the vinegar will not rust the lid shut. Discard the fruit solids. The shrub is now ready for use and can be kept in the refrigerator.

★ Cider Shrub Love Potion* ★

This potion can be consumed by one or more people to infuse themselves with loving and love-attracting vibrations and can also be used as a libation in other love magic.

Items Needed

1 orange, quartered

2 cups unsweetened apple juice or cider

1 teaspoon pumpkin pie spice

1 tablespoon brown sugar

¼ cup Love Shrub mixture

Empower each ingredient for love. Leaving the peel intact, wash the orange and then cut it into four pieces. Remove the stem. Place the orange in a cauldron along with the apple juice, spices, and brown sugar. Warm this over medium heat, covered. Once the cider begins to simmer, turn the heat down to low and let it mull for twenty minutes. When the time is up, remove the cauldron from heat and let the cider cool. When it has cooled, strain it and stir in the shrub. This recipe can be adjusted to individual taste, adding more apple juice if too sweet or more sugar if too tart. The potion is now ready to use and can be served either hot or cold, reheating if needed.

((●))

Though this next potion could technically be classified as an elixir—it is a sweetened mixture with both water and alcohol—it is perfectly suited for deep, emotional love. It is similar to the cider potion but with the inclusion of red wine.

★ True Love Mulled Wine* ★

Items Needed

½ cup water

1 pinch nutmeg

1 pinch ginger

3 cinnamon sticks, broken

1 bottle (750ml) red wine

1 apple, coarsely chopped

¼ cup Love Shrub mixture

Empower the ingredients for love. Pour the water in the cauldron and over low heat carefully simmer the herbs in the water for a few moments until you can smell them in the air. Add the wine to this mixture and the apples and simmer it all over low heat for at least twenty minutes and up to three hours. After this mulling, remove the wine from heat and allow it to cool. Strain the apples and spices out of the wine, then stir in the shrub mixture. The wine is ready to serve.

ꪜꪜ●꪿꪿

Even though there is wine in more than one of these recipes, I do not wish to imply that in order to have a proper love potion one needs to consume alcohol. There are definite alternatives available for those who do not wish to use alcohol, or if you just don't care for red wine.

★ True Love's Kiss Potion (Alcohol-free) ★
Items Needed

1 cup water

½ cup red rose petals, bruised

½ cup crushed vervain leaves

¼ cup coconut oil

Empower the coconut oil with the pure desire for true love and bright pink light. Empower the herbs with your desire for love as well with red and pink light and the full passion of your desire. Simmer the herbs in the water in the usual manner and then allow the liquid to cool. Once cooled add a few drops of the potion-water to the coconut oil and stir to mix.

To use: Very lightly anoint your lips with the coconut oil in the manner of a lip balm. It can also be used (again, very lightly) to moisturize the hands. This will attract compatible partners and when love is felt, a kiss of your anointed lips shall seal the deal.

★ Cooling-Off Potion ★

Though finding love can be a wonderful experience filled with romance and boundless joy, there are points along that journey that can be filled with boredom, unease, or sheer revulsion. It is for those times that a potion to quell passion and love feelings could be helpful. Admittedly, the administration of this one does straddle the ethical boundaries but considering that it does not cause harm—it simply eases the process of separation—I felt that it should be included here.

Items Needed

½ cup roasted pistachios

½ cup water

2 teaspoons lavender

½ cup chopped or shredded cucumber

2 hearts of lettuce, chopped

½ cup lemon juice

½ teaspoon salt

Charge each of the ingredients with the intention of calming passion and peaceful separation. In a food processor or blender, grind up the pistachios. They will start to get a peanut butter-like consistency and that is fine. In the cauldron, add the water, lavender, cucumber, and lettuce hearts and bring them to a simmer. After the water starts to bubble and steam, turn off the heat and cover. Leave for at least fifteen minutes to cool. During that time, combine the pistachio mixture, lemon juice, and salt in a big bowl. Once the lettuce and lavender brew has cooled, strain the liquid into the pistachio mixture, whisking to thoroughly blend. The resulting potion will be relatively creamy, which makes the next part easier.

To use: The simplest method of administering this potion is through the clever repurposing of a salad. You can quickly turn the potion into a vinaigrette dressing with the addition of ½ cup olive oil and 3 tablespoons apple cider vinegar, again whisking to blend and then pour over a light green salad and share it with the target of the magic … unless they have a nut allergy, of course! If they do, omit the pistachios and double the amount of lettuce hearts but keep in mind the taste and texture will be altered considerably.

The hitch with this recipe is that it must be *shared* with the person, as the potion acts to free *both* parties from each other. Warning: This is meant to be used for the highest good and *not* to cause harm by attempting to end someone else's happy relationship. Trying to "make" someone leave their partner to be with you instead is unlikely to work anyway, as this potion requires at least one party to have the desire to separate from the other in order to be effective.

Money

Second only to love magic are the spells, potions, and charms related to the pursuit of money or prosperity. Though more related to mundane matters, wealth is a fine magical goal. In my opinion, the magical community has too often been guided into thinking that working for tangible items is somehow dishonorable or unspiritual. I think that viewpoint is incorrect and only serves to keep us in a state of lack. To my mind, if we are to fully embrace our everyday lives alongside our spiritual callings, there must be balance. To accept the idea that we have the power to alter reality through magic but then forego using it to meet our earthly needs is to reject half of our potential. In the Witchcraft I practice, the idea that one needs to give up their worldly possession or live in forced poverty to somehow prove a superior level of spirituality or "awareness" is not at all accepted. Money and other mundane things can be the subject of magical workings without judgement. The other extreme is obsession with financial accumulation, which is not a spiritual pursuit; excess wealth and extreme poverty are both unnatural states on the opposite ends of the same spectrum. The bottom line is that using magic for personal gain and money is perfectly acceptable. And to that end, it is best for the gain not to come from the misfortune of others or the primary focus or obsession to have wealth for wealth's sake. Personally, I have never seen any virtue in endless struggle, needless suffering, or excessive self-denial. My belief is that ensuring our needs are met frees us to focus on higher goals.

★ Money Magnet Potion ★

Drinking this potion and anointing it on paper money helps to align ourselves with the energies of growth, expansion, and abundance, the closest magical energies to money. Money itself is an artificial creation of humanity, so it can only carry the energy we assign to it.

Items Needed

2 cups water

1 tablespoon sunflower seeds

1 tablespoon lemon peel

1 tablespoon chamomile

1 tablespoon cinquefoil (five-finger grass)

1 teaspoon woodruff

¼ teaspoon yellow mustard seed

Stevia, to taste

Empower each of the ingredients for money and brew in the usual manner. Once the potion has cooled and been strained, drink a cupful sweetened if desired. Stevia is the recommended sweetener for money potions as this herb is aligned with money and success magic.

《《●》》

The previous potion aims for a magnetic-like attraction ability to draw in the proper opportunities and situations to generate more money, but that process is best for long-term security. If immediate need has reared its ugly head, then a more fast-acting (but shorter term) potion might be the better option. This formula is similar in power and energy to what are usually called "Fast Luck Oils" and can produce some pretty strong results rather quickly.

★ Fast Money Potion* ★

Items Needed

  2 cups water

  1 tablespoon cinnamon

  1 tablespoon vanilla extract

  2 teaspoons peppermint

  1 teaspoon spearmint

  Stevia, to taste

Empower each ingredient to attract money then brew as usual. Sweeten with Stevia if desired. In addition to drinking the potion to activate the magic, gold or silver jewelry can also be soaked overnight in the unsweetened liquid to magically charge it, thus creating a wearable money talisman.

CC●))

Though potions are drinkable, the brews presented here are not. However, they do have a variety of uses, including this first one, to bathe yourself in the power of abundance.

★ Money Bath Brew ★

Items Needed

2 cups water

1 tablespoon basil

1 tablespoon patchouli

1 tablespoon sunflower seeds

1 teaspoon chamomile

1 teaspoon peppermint

1 teaspoon allspice

¼ teaspoon cloves

Empower the ingredients and brew in the usual way. Allow this brew to cool for twenty minutes and then strain it into a large cup (preferably a plastic container you can take with you into the bathroom). Once strained, add the brew to a bath. As you soak in it, envision yourself prosperous and happy, remembering to feel the way you want to feel when your magical goal is achieved.

★ Floor Wash Brew for Financial Security ★

This brew recipe is specifically aimed at cleansing and charging the floors of your home or business with power to attract abundance. Before using, however, it is important to make sure your floor is not easily damaged; do not use this wash on delicate floors or carpeting.

Items Needed

  2 cups water

  1 tablespoon fenugreek seeds

  1 tablespoon chopped fresh basil

Empower the ingredients for abundance and growth and brew in the usual manner. Once the brew has cooled and been strained, add it to the regular scrub water you would use to clean your floors. Clean your floors and also just outside your front door to invite prosperity inside.

Luck

Luck magic is a curious thing to me. For a while in my youth, I was very much focused on trying to understand the nature of luck and chance; at the time, I considered myself "unlucky" and desperately sought to remedy my situation. After quite a bit of research, contemplation, and consultation with others wiser than I was, I came to a few understandings about what we call luck. I think that luck is really a matter of a few factors working in harmony. The first factor is a somewhat heightened intuition that allows for making better choices, such that it appears opportunities just arrive out of thin air. The second factor is a good level of protection, a strong aura that helps shield and ward off potential dangers. The third factor is a strong enough level of self-esteem and confidence that a person doesn't unintentionally invite misfortune. I think one of the reasons the energy of the planet Jupiter is aligned with luck is that the expansion, success, and influence power Jupiter naturally carries helps to manifest all three of these factors within an individual. The following recipes carry the magic to aid in the cultivation of the necessary qualities that make a person lucky.

★ Good Luck Potion* ★

Items Needed

1½ cups water

1 tablespoon spearmint

1 tablespoon bergamot mint (see note in recipe)

1 tablespoon lemongrass

½ cup pineapple juice

Empower the ingredients and simmer the herbs in the water until steam rises and bubbles form in the bottom of the cauldron. Remove from heat, cover the pot, and allow to cool for at least ten minutes. Once the potion has cooled, strain it into a large cup and add the pineapple juice. Drink it while envisioning yourself surrounded by bright green or medium blue light. Please note that bergamot mint is a member of the mint family that is frequently available fresh in supermarkets in the summertime (at least in my region), though its availability may vary. It is also sometimes called orange mint, Eau de Cologne mint, *Mentha aquatica* var. *citrata* or *M. citrate*. I have even seen *M. citrata* called "chocolate mint" here and there; either way, it is the same herb. If it cannot be found fresh, check the tea aisle.

★ Lucky Citrus Spice Potion* ★

This potion helps to improve good fortune and is light and refreshing in flavor.

Items Needed

1 cup water

1 teaspoon lemon zest

½ teaspoon orange zest

¼ teaspoon nutmeg

¼ teaspoon allspice

1 cup orange juice

Sweetener (sugar, Stevia, or honey), to taste

Ice

Empower the ingredients for luck and brew the zest and spices in the water in the usual manner. Once the potion has been cooled and strained, add the orange juice, sugar (or other sweetener), and the ice. Drink to shift your personal energy to a luckier vibration.

$$((\bullet))$$

Part of what is considered luck is related to success in any chosen endeavor. The following brew helps to tip the scales in our favor. It can be used in the bath, to anoint talismans for luck, as a floor wash to keep the environment attuned to your good fortune, or poured into a witch bottle and sealed to radiate its power like a magical battery—but definitely do not drink it.

★ Luck and Influence Brew ★

Items Needed

2 cups water

2 tablespoon high John the conqueror root

1 teaspoon frankincense

1 teaspoon myrrh

1 teaspoon allspice

1 teaspoon lemongrass

Empower the ingredients for luck and influence and brew in the usual manner. After the brew has cooled, strain it and pour it into a jar with a tight-fitting lid for use.

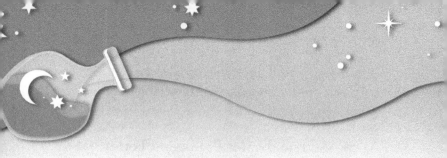

Chapter 7
PROTECTION POTIONS AND BREWS

Whether for an extra boost of security while traveling or for safety in everyday life, magical forms of protection are a very common goal of many forms of practice, and potion-making is no exception. In fact, protection potions and brews are an excellent method of conferring a protective energy to a high degree; infusing yourself with this power on a cellular level. Depending upon the potion, these can be used to aid physical protection from danger and harm, protection from accidents, and also spiritual and magical protection from psychic attack or malevolent creatures.

The potion recipes are all safe to drink (as long as there are no allergies to any of the ingredients) and can be used as often as needed unless otherwise noted. One of the common culinary herbs that is a powerful protectant (among other things) is basil. It protects on all levels. Whether harm may come on the physical, mental, or magical planes, basil will help to neutralize or block it from reaching you.

★ Herb and Spice Protection Potion* ★

This potion uses the power of basil and adds other herbs known to provide strong defense against all sorts of danger.

Items Needed

  2 cups water

  1 tablespoon basil

  1 tablespoon fennel

  1 tablespoon anise seeds

  1 tablespoon lime juice

  1 teaspoon fresh lemon zest

  1 tablespoon sugar (or chosen sweetener)

Empower each ingredient with protective intention and power. Add the water to the cauldron along with the next three ingredients and brew in the usual way. Remove from heat and then add the lime juice, lemon zest, and sugar, stirring to mix. Strain the potion into cups and sip to become infused with protective energy. Mentally envision yourself being filled and surrounded with a powerful silver-white light that forms an impenetrable shield of protection around you.

((●))

Though not an inherently protective substance, coffee does possess the qualities of clarity and power enhancement, making it a boost to any magical working. Using it as a base for a potion gives the resulting creation more energy and a stronger focus—a definite plus when making something to grant protection. Though a great many people have enjoyed this coffee-based potion (during autumn it is ubiquitous), most aren't aware of its full magical potential.

★ Pumpkin Spice Coffee Protection* ★

Not only can this mixture be made right at home for protective purposes but the coffee shop version can be empowered for the same purpose (though I think the homemade version is strongest).

Items Needed

1 cup milk

1 tablespoon pumpkin puree (optional)

2 teaspoons light brown sugar

1 teaspoon vanilla extract

¼ teaspoon pumpkin pie spice

½ cup strong coffee

Though there are variations in recipes, as far as I am concerned the best version of pumpkin pie spice is a blend of the following: 1 tablespoon cinnamon, 1 teaspoon nutmeg, 1 teaspoon ginger, 2 teaspoons allspice, and ½ teaspoon cloves. This can be mixed together in advance and used in baking and potions as needed. The spice mixture is powerful and can be charged for love, protection, and healing. Though this version is the one I used in the recipe, a store-bought blend can be used instead if need be. Returning to the recipe at hand, empower each of the ingredients for protection. In the cauldron over medium heat, warm the milk (and the pumpkin puree, if using) and the light brown sugar, whisking to blend. Keep stirring until the milk begins to steam, being careful to avoid boiling it. When the steam has risen, remove from heat and whisk in the vanilla and ¼ teaspoon of the pumpkin pie spice. Whisk in the coffee until blended and frothy. Drink as desired to infuse yourself with protection.

★ Cloak of the Dark Goddess ★
Protection Potion

Not only does this potion contain herbs that are highly protective in nature, they are also aligned with dark goddess energy. The mixture brings magical protection and can also be used to help connect with dark goddesses, though the potion is still effective even without divine assistance.

Items Needed

2 cups water

½ cup blackberries

1 tablespoon dried dark red rose petals

1 tablespoon elder flowers

1 teaspoon mint

¼ teaspoon mugwort

Pinch wormwood

Garlic peels (optional)

Empower the ingredients and if you wish, call upon a dark goddess with whom you have an affinity, asking that she bestow protective power into the potion. Next, brew in the usual manner, muddling the blackberries into the water before adding the herbs. The garlic peels are included to help align with the power of Hecate specifically without imparting a heavy garlic flavor. If you are not calling upon her, they can be omitted. Once the potion has cooled, strain and sweeten it as desired and as you drink focus on the chosen dark goddess and again ask for protection (if desired). Though it is better to call on deities only if you have a preexisting relationship with them, some examples of goddesses considered dark include the Cailleach, the Morrigan, Hecate, Hel, Kali, Lilith, and Sekhmet.

《（●）》

Though some potions from long ago contain bothersome, unsavory, or even currently unidentifiable ingredients, other potions created and used centuries ago are remarkably simple. The following easy potion offers protection from malevolent otherworldly beings and forces as well as mundane dangers such as accidents.

★ Sassafras Protection Potion ★

In addition to being a powerful protectant, this potion can also be used to bring money or healing. The recipe can remain the same; simply charge the potion with the type of intention best suited to your needs at the time of making.

Items Needed

4 cups water

¼ cup chopped sassafras roots

Pinch salt

Honey, to taste

Charge the roots for protection and add them and the water to a cauldron. Bring the water to a boil and let the potion bubble for fifteen minutes. Next, remove from heat, add a pinch of salt, cover and allow the liquid to cool until it is drinkable, five to fifteen minutes depending. Pour a cup of the potion and add some honey to sweeten it to your liking. Sip it slowly feeling its energy merge with your own to create an aura of protection over, around, and throughout your body.

★ Green Herb Protection Potion* ★

This green herb protection potion is powerful without being too heavy. The recipe offers enhanced personal safety with the added convenience of requiring only four ingredients, three of which can be found in the spice aisle of any supermarket.

Items Needed

    2 cups water

    1 tablespoon rosemary

    1 tablespoon peppermint

    1 tablespoon parsley

Empower the herbs for protection and brew in the usual way. Once the potion has cooled, strain it and drink a cup of it to absorb its protective power. As with the Herb and Spice Protection Potion, you can mentally envision yourself being filled and surrounded with a powerful silver-white light forming an impenetrable shield of protection around you to fully focus the potion's magic.

★ Potion of Protection and Strength ★

If your protection needs also require a boost of strength, this recipe should provide the added power that is needed.

Items Needed

2 cups water

1 tablespoon white oak bark

1 apple, cored and chopped

1 tablespoon rosemary

1 teaspoon vanilla extract

Empower the ingredients for protection. Boil the oak bark in the water for fifteen minutes then remove from heat and add the remaining ingredients. Cover the pot and allow the potion to steep for ten more minutes. Strain the liquid and sip a cup of it to fill yourself with protection energy and improved inner strength.

$($ $($ ● $)$ $)$

The power of protection can reach much further beyond the personal; these next recipes are brews that can serve as powerful protectants for the home, vehicle, or any space that needs to be safeguarded.

★ Protection Brew ★

This is a very powerful mixture that makes use of sacred resins and highly protective herbs. Though frankincense is called for in this recipe, since it is becoming rarer and somewhat endangered, an excellent substitute is 1 tablespoon of cut or ground pine needles. I just hold a bunch of fresh pine needles in my hand and trim them into tiny bits with shears over a plate until I have the required amount.

Items Needed

2 cups water

1 tablespoon frankincense (or pine needles)

1 tablespoon myrrh

1 tablespoon nettle

1 tablespoon black cohosh

1 tablespoon copal

Empower the ingredients for protection and brew in the usual way. Allow the brew to cool and then strain it.

To use: This brew can be added to wash water for floors, poured down kitchen and bathroom drains, sprinkled under the welcome mat at the front door to keep danger at bay, or used to wash the car tires to provide vehicle security.

☾☽

A very simple brew to infuse your clothing with protective power only uses two ingredients: black cohosh and water.

★ Protective Fabric Brew ★

Black cohosh is frequently used as an herbal supplement, which makes it easier to find. If necessary, you can break open capsules of the raw herb supplement to gather enough for the brew. Black cohosh is sometimes also known as black snake root.

Items Needed

2 cups water

4 tablespoons black cohosh

Empower the herb for protection. Boil the black cohosh in the water for fifteen minutes then remove from heat and allow it to cool completely. Thoroughly strain the brew and then add it to the washing machine when you wash the chosen clothing. Whichever clothing you choose, it is best if it is sturdy and dark colored, both for symbolic reasons and to make sure that delicate clothing is not stained or otherwise damaged by the brew. The clothes are then washed and dried as usual. Then when they are worn, they offer protection to the wearer.

))●((

Any of the potions or brews that have been featured in this chapter can be used before ritual workings or psychic sessions to help keep yourself safe from any incorrect energies or harmful beings. With protection taken care of, most types of magical work can then be conducted with confidence and a reasonable assurance of safety.

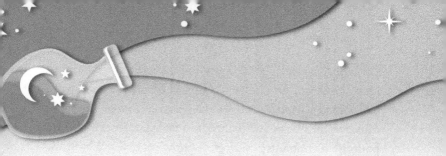

Chapter 8
PSYCHIC POTIONS
AND DIVINATION BREWS

O ne of the many stereotypes regarding Witches' potions and brews is that we bubble up some secret mixture in the cauldron to discover hidden knowledge or connect with the other side. Luckily for us, this particular stereotype has much more than just a kernel of truth behind it; there are indeed many potions and brews for psychic enhancement and divination. Some of the potions included here help to relax the logical mind so that the psychic mind can have greater prominence while others help in the contact of outside forces so that they may reveal prophecy or other information.

This first potion is one based on a legendary Welsh potion made by the goddess Cerridwen herself. It is said that in order to create a powerful potion of Awen, she read books of astronomy and planetary hours and gathered charm-bearing herbs for a year and a day. During her gathering, she had a boy named Gwion Bach as her helper to stir the potion in the cauldron, but he accidentally consumed the last drops of the potion which granted him great knowledge. Cerridwen was understandably upset that her work had been spoiled and a magical battle ensued between the two. Eventually, she ate him and he was reborn as the great bard, Taliesin. Awen is the "flowing spirit" that can bestow knowledge and inspiration and it is this energy from which Gwion Bach was given his newfound ability. From this we see the power of inspiration, and it is this ancient tale that inspired this modern potion, which was originally featured in one of my previous works.

★ Cauldron of Inspiration Potion* ★

Each herb in this recipe is linked to one of the major planetary bodies acknowledged in astrology; each may be called upon to lend their energies to the greater whole.

Items Needed

2 cups water

1 teaspoon rosemary (Sun)

1 teaspoon sage (Jupiter)

1 teaspoon mint (Mercury)

1 teaspoon grapefruit zest (Saturn)

1 teaspoon basil (Mars)

1 teaspoon lemon juice (Moon)

1 tablespoon honey (Venus)

Charge each of the herbs and the honey separately for inspiration. In a cauldron or pot, heat the water to just under the boiling point when steam begins to rise. Add the herbs one at a time, and allow the brew to come to a boil. After the pot is fully boiling, turn off the heat and cover the pot. Allow the brew to steep and cool for at least fifteen minutes. Uncover the pot and stir in the honey. Pour a cup of the brew, straining it if necessary, and relax as you take slow sips of the potion allowing your mind to open to wisdom. This potion can be used not only to find inspiration but also to expand the consciousness to greater forces and the unknown allowing you to discover that which may be hidden.

★ Third Eye Potion ★

This recipe helps to stimulate clairvoyant (clear sight) ability to glimpse into the unknown.

Items Needed

2 cups water

1 tablespoon rose petals

1 tablespoon yarrow

½ teaspoon cinnamon

½ teaspoon mugwort

Pinch nutmeg

Sweetener (sugar, Stevia, or honey), to taste

Empower the herbs for psychic vision and brew in the usual way. Once the potion has cooled, strain and sweeten as desired. Drink a cup while in a relaxed restful state and attempt to envision the answers you seek. Keep notes of your impressions, which may be symbolic and in need of later interpretation.

((●))

While the previous two potions focused on reaching the mind's eye (and ear), the next potion is focused on awakening the physical sight via the art of scrying. This is the practice of gazing into a surface such as a dark mirror, water, ink, a crystal, et cetera, in order to "see" images or scenes on or within the surface of the gazing tool. It is also possible to see things within the mind while doing this work; using a tool of focus can help induce the light trance state ideal for psychic work.

★ Scrying Potion ★

This magical beverage is a scrying standard and no book of Witch's potions would be complete without a version of it.

Items Needed

    2 cups water

    1 tablespoon mugwort

    ½ teaspoon wormwood

    Sweetener (sugar, Stevia, or honey), to taste

Charge the herbs and boil the water. Once the water has begun to boil, add the herbs and cover, turning off the heat and allowing them to steep for ten minutes. Next, strain the potion, sweetening as desired and slowly sip a cupful of the drink, relaxing and finishing the cup before you begin to scry.

$$\complement\complement\bullet\supset\supset$$

One of the classic methods of contacting the psychic mind to divine future events or uncover hidden truths via the use of a brewed drink is tasseography or reading tea leaves. Though regular black tea (a fermented and roasted form of green tea) can be used for this purpose, its main magical associations are courage, money, and lust. To my mind, a more effective choice would be to use an herbal potion blend specifically designed to aid psychic awareness in tasseography rather than using plain tea. The version of tea known as "white tea," which is really delicate immature green tea, handpicked early and dried quickly to preserve the freshest flavor, has magical associations with fertility, balance, renewal, clarity, and psychic ability and as such is an excellent choice for the work at hand.

★ Tasseography Potion ★

The word "tasseography" refers to divination by means of reading patterns in tea leaves, coffee grounds, and other mixtures. This potion uses tea and other herbs to provide a means for the patterns to form.

Items Needed

    2 cups water

    1 teaspoon white tea

    ½ teaspoon yarrow

    ¼ teaspoon mugwort

Empower the ingredients to tap the psychic mind and to read true. Heat the water until it begins to steam and then remove it from the heat. At this point, add the herbs and cover for at least three but no more than ten minutes. If you want to focus on a question or a specific time period, focus on this when preparing and drinking the potion. If you are reading for another person, have them focus on what they wish to cover while you are preparing and while they sip the potion.

Reading the Tea

First, choose a tea cup without any decorations on the inside of it so as not to hinder the reading. Additionally, make sure to have a saucer or plate on which to overturn the cup when necessary. After the potion has brewed, stir it lightly and ladle some into the tea cup, making sure to include some of the leaves and sweeten lightly if desired. After drinking the tea until there is only a slight amount of liquid left in the bottom of the cup, the cup is swirled, often three times in a clockwise motion and then the cup is quickly overturned onto the saucer and then turned upright once again. The way I do it, the images deciphered near the rim of the cup related to the now, those found in the middle areas relate to the near future and the ones found at the bottom of the cup relate to the distant future. If you are doing a reading for the past then the top is still the now or just passed, the middle is the recent past and the bottom is the distant past. To read the leaves, look at the patterns that appear to be formed in the cup. It is very helpful to have a notebook and pen handy. Perhaps draw a wide half oval to represent the teacup and jot down notations of the symbols you see on the paper where you see them in the cup. This will make for easier interpretation. You may see numbers, letters, or symbols in the cup and these can then be interpreted in regards to a question or simply to life in general.

Some of the most commonly seen symbols and their meanings are:

Arrow: Direction and movement; the direction in which the arrow is pointing and any symbols that appear close to it provide clarification

Bell: An alert, expect news

Bird: Freedom, flight, travel

Circles: Wholeness, balance, gifts, money

Clouds: Trouble, clouded judgement

Coins or paper money: Financial changes—look to nearby symbols for insight

Cup (or cauldron): Emotions, love, what you value

Doors: Beginnings or endings, opening or closing; look to nearby symbols for clarification

Eyes: Vision, clairvoyance, seeing clearly, sometimes being watched

Flowers or leaves: Nature, growth, hope, advancement

Hands: Help, friendship, partnership

Heart: Love, emotion, good feelings

Horseshoe: Luck

Key: Opportunities, unlocking doors

Kite: Hopes, wishes

Letters: These can be initials or clarifying clues for other symbols

Lines: Direction and travel; the longer the line is, the greater the length of the trip

Moon: Intuition, hidden things, subconscious mind

Needle or spear: Making a point, action, willpower, recognition

Numbers: These can indicate increments of time or amount of people or objects

Question mark: Questions and uncertainty

Runes and other magical symbols: Usually indicates their traditional meanings; consult books of symbols for interpretation

Star or pentagram: Happiness, power, and magic, especially if the star is within a circle

Sun: Happiness, expansion, conscious mind

Sword (or knife): Thoughts, skill, alertness, conflict

Zodiac symbols: These and other astrological symbols can indicate people or the time of year in which an event takes place

After all the symbols have been uncovered and recorded, they can be interpreted according to the framework of the reading and their placement in the cup. Be sure to write down any additional impressions you receive beyond the meanings given here, as the potion will help to add a level of depth and specificity to the reading.

(()>)

Sometimes we don't necessarily want a powerful psychic experience but just one where we quiet the mind a bit and relax. If you have trouble relaxing or mediating, the next recipe is very helpful.

★ Meditation Potion ★

These ingredients all carry a calming and meditative energy that helps all meditative work.

Items Needed

    2 cups water

    1 teaspoon hibiscus

    ½ teaspoon yarrow

    ½ teaspoon lavender

    ½ teaspoon chamomile

    Honey, to taste

Empower the herbs with lavender light energy for meditation and calm. Brew in the usual manner. After the potion has cooled and been strained, sweeten with honey as desired. Sip as warm as possible (without burning your mouth), then relax and attempt meditation.

The Green Fairy

"Green fairy" is a nickname for absinthe, the anise-flavored wormwood spirit that has been used as a visionary potion for generations. Though it has been illegal in places over the years due to the fear that it may cause madness or other side effects when abused, it has continued to be manufactured and used into modern times. Now, it *is* illegal to distill your own liquor but a perfectly legal and acceptable alternative is to infuse a clear liquor with the herbs and thus make a homemade green fairy to aid visionary, ritual, and psychic work without the threat of arrest or the high prices and hassle of trying to purchase the commercial variety. An easy recipe for green fairy, this blend yields a light green drink that can be used in the traditional manner of absinthe: one part green fairy poured into a glass and two or three parts iced water poured slowly into it over a sugar cube on a slotted spoon held over the glass. If properly done, the liquid will turn from light green to a milky color but is still ready to drink even if not.

★ Green Fairy Potion ★

Items Needed

3 cups vodka

6 tablespoons wormwood

½ cup mint leaves (or 4 tablespoons mint extract)

¼ cup anise seeds (or 2 tablespoons anise extract)

Empower the ingredients and combine everything in a jar with a tight-fitting lid or a corked jar (that must then be sealed with candle wax). Allow the mixture to steep for seven days out of direct light, shaking the mixture once a day. After the seventh day, strain the liquid from the herbs and rebottle for use.

To use: For one easy serving, add 2 tablespoons green fairy to a small glass and pour ¼ cup ice water through a slotted absinthe spoon with a sugar cube placed on it. Sip the potion, and then you are ready for your usual psychic or ritual work.

))●((

Though psychic potions help align the mind to better attune to the unknown and unseen realms, brews for psychic and divinatory work can offer their energy in a different way. They help by enhancing the external portion of the work. This first brew adds an extra boost of power to water scrying.

★ Darkness and Light Scrying Brew ★

The ingredients in this brew not only provide a magical power boost to help scrying, but they also create a dark liquid which provides a wonderful scrying surface.

Items Needed

> 1 cup water
>
> 4 tablespoons mugwort
>
> ½ cup unsweetened cherry juice
>
> ½ cup unsweetened pomegranate juice
>
> 1 small piece of silver (such as a ring, coin, cufflink, earring)

Empower the ingredients for psychic power and simmer the mugwort in the water just until it begins to boil. Remove from heat and add the cherry and pomegranate juices. Once the brew has cooled, strain it and return it to the cauldron. Add the piece of silver and take the cauldron to a table near a comfortable chair. Peer into the liquid and scry for any answers that you seek, making sure to record any impressions you receive in a notebook for further interpretation.

((●))

Another method of using brews in psychic work is to prepare the environment by charging the atmosphere with power. Whether or not you cast a circle in your practice, this brew can be used to sprinkle around your working area to create a more inviting energy for psychic phenomena to manifest. One word of caution: make sure that the floor of the working area can get wet without damage. And note that because sandalwood is becoming endangered, cedar makes a fine substitute.

★ Psychic Circle Brew ★

Items Needed

2 cups water

1 tablespoon mugwort

1 tablespoon lavender

1 tablespoon sandalwood (or cedar)

1 teaspoon white willow bark

1 teaspoon coriander

1 teaspoon cardamom

Empower the herbs for psychic power and brew in the standard way. When the brew has cooled, strain some into a chalice and use it to asperge (sprinkle) a circle around your working area. If you cast a traditional circle, this brew can be used in place of the salt and water in the rite. After casting, any psychic or divinatory work can be done within this circle to a greater advantage.

Whether you choose to use green fairy alcohol or want to read tea leaves, each of these potions offers their unique ability to tap into the psychic part of our minds and help reveal the unknown. The brews listed here offer a means of creating a better environment to manifest answers from the hidden realms. We can use these recipes to increase our spirituality, making ourselves more aware of the otherworldly realities underlying our physical world.

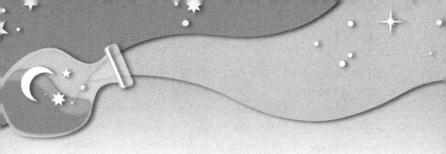

Chapter 9
POTIONS AND BREWS FOR
THE SABBATS AND ESBATS

You know what's fun? Stirring a cauldron filled with a bubbling potion as the sun sets on a crisp Samhain night. As the ingredients brew together and thoughts turn to the upcoming festivities, the urge to cackle is almost inescapable. And when the Yuletide potion is simmering and the fragrant steam fills the room, releasing a special winter magic in the air that charges the atmosphere with ideal holiday energy in preparation of the ritual to follow, or when creating any of the potions in this chapter, the feelings of joy and wonderfully Witchy satisfaction are both inspiring and powerful magical boosts to celebrating any sabbat or esbat.

There are countless books and websites that cover the rich lore and practice of each sabbat and esbat, so I won't go too far into the history or rituals of the holidays. I will instead focus on the potion recipes that can be incorporated into any ritual practice, either as enhancement to an existing rite or simply a method of attunement to the day's overall energy. Let's look at the sabbats first and follow with recipes for several types of esbat.

Samhain

Whether you choose to celebrate this holiday on Halloween, October 31, or the full moon in the zodiac sign of Taurus (with the sun in Scorpio), or when the sun is positioned at 15 degrees in Scorpio (known to some as "astrological Samhain"), or on any other date, it makes little difference as to the sabbat's overall meaning. Considered the "final harvest," Samhain was considered the meat harvest in the old days when herds were culled, leaving only the strongest animals alive to conserve resources and for survivability through the winter. Samhain is also known as a time to honor the ancestors and departed loved ones, and it is taught that the mists or veil between worlds is thinner at this time, making it easier to connect with the Otherworld. Individual traditions have a great deal of lore associated with this day in particular but one theme that appears consistently is of transformation. Be it in acknowledging death, the harvest, the coming of winter, the passing of the harvest lord, or the changing of one year to another, transformation is a deep underlying concept.

The energy found during Samhain can be extremely powerful; some say it is the most magical sabbat of the year. With these understandings in mind, it becomes clear that any magical actions undertaken now carry with them a special significance and should be carefully chosen and crafted, especially if our ancestors and deities are paying extra close attention during this time. Not only is it important to have a clear focus on our goals and celebrations during Samhain, it is perhaps equally important to take sensible precautions against any potential malevolent Otherworldly forces that may come to do harm at this time of greater movement between realms. When properly constructed and magically charged, traditional crafts such as the jack-o'-Lantern offer good protection against wandering spirits and other forms of trouble. Additionally, potions and brews can aid in this purpose. To keep the proper energy and atmosphere, this Samhain potion aligns the power to that of the sabbat and also offers protection against any who would have harmful intentions.

★ Samhain Nexus Potion* ★

A nexus is a point through which energy is drawn, an X that marks the spot. Sacred places of energy and power found throughout the world are essentially nexus points through which spiritual energies pass.

Items Needed

1 cup water

1 quart of blackberries (or 1 cup juice)

1 teaspoon black tea (or 1 tea bag)

1 tablespoon grated beet

¼ teaspoon sage

¼ teaspoon rosemary

Empower each ingredient before using. As you are charging this potion, envision power coming from only the most correct and beneficial energies of the universe to empower the liquid and that it will serve as a drink to align with the energies of Samhain and protect those who drink it. If you are using fresh blackberries, add them to the water first; after the water has warmed for a few minutes, crush the berries with a spoon or fork in the water to release the juice. Add the rest of the ingredients and brew in the usual manner. Once cooled, strain the liquid and drink as desired to attune with the day or use it in place of wine for the ritual libation.

((●))

The brew featured for Samhain provides an inviting atmosphere for Otherworldly beings you may wish to visit while at the same time bars those who might cause disruption or harm.

★ Hallows Night Brew ★

The ingredients in this brew are each aligned with Samhain and autumn and offer energies that create the perfect atmosphere for the magic and rituals which are conducted at this time.

Items Needed

2 cups water

2 tablespoons wormwood

2 tablespoons tarragon

2 tablespoons rosemary

2 tablespoons sage

1 teaspoon cloves

1 apple, chopped

Personal item from each person attending (optional)

The "personal item" from each person attending the Samhain sabbat could be a single hair, a drop of blood, a nail clipping, or a tiny bit of saliva, offered reverently. These are used to connect the participants with the sabbat's otherworldly energies but can be omitted if preferred. Either way, each of the ingredients is empowered and then everything is added to the cauldron and the mixture is boiled, uncovered, to allow the steam to permeate the area. Remove from the heat and allow the cauldron to cool enough that it can be carried. If you are working the ritual outdoors, the brew can be poured out in a circle around the ritual area. If working indoors, the cauldron of brew can either be placed by the front door of the home to release its power or in the western quadrant of the ritual space.

Yule

The winter solstice is an absolutely magical time when the chill of winter and the longest night of the year offer the hidden promise of the return of warmth and light. From this point forward there will be an increase in light by approximately one minute per day all the way until the summer solstice, so even though we stand in the midst of the coldest and darkest part of the year, we can be assured that the cycle continues and the light half of the year draws steadily closer. An underlying theme for this sabbat is rebirth; the birth and rebirth of many deities as well as the rebirth and renewal of the solar cycle. What little greenery can be found in nature now reminds us that life and magic can persevere even in the harshest of times and in so doing helps lay the groundwork for the time of abundance to follow.

Yule's energy is the hinge of the year, the critical time when the earth seems to stand still for a moment. And when it begins to move again, everything has changed though we may not yet be able to perceive it. We very often focus our magic and celebrations on this change with festivities centered on warmth, light, hope, and the slowly returning heat of the sun.

★ Yuletide Wheel Potion ★

The potion for this sabbat offers a drinkable version of this energy which attunes our bodies and minds to the magic of this time and helps us to tap into the sacred powers of both the sun and the earth present during this beautiful holiday.

Items Needed

2 cups water

1 tablespoon rosemary

1 tablespoon orange zest

3 cinnamon sticks, broken

½ teaspoon juniper berries

Empower the herbs and brew the potion in the usual way. Once cooled and strained, this potion can be used in the place of wine in ritual or drunk before a rite to enhance a connection with Yule's energy. The brew offered here has a bright, enchanting vibration that fills the area with liveliness that is perfectly attuned to this sabbat's power.

★ Yuletide Renewal Brew ★

With sprigs of evergreen and fragrant herbs, this brew is truly in alignment with all of the delicate yet potent magic of this special day.

Items Needed

2 cups water

¼ cup cranberries

2 tablespoons rosemary

2 tablespoons orange zest

2 tablespoons peppermint

½ teaspoon cinnamon

1 sprig of fir

1 sprig of pine

1 holly leaf (optional)

1 ivy leaf (optional)

Empower each ingredient to attune with the power of the sabbat and brew slowly over low heat, uncovered so steam releases into the area. Again, if you are going to work ritual outdoors, this brew (once cooled and strained) can be poured in a circle around the working site. If indoors, it can be placed by the front door, set beside the hearth, or left on the stove to continue to invite in the season's energy.

Imbolc

Though some have argued that it is redundant to celebrate all eight sabbats—the quarters and cross-quarters are both supposed to acknowledge the standard four seasons found in a year—it is easy to find value in keeping all eight upon looking more deeply. A perfect example of this view is in the magic of Imbolc. While the winter solstice explores the theme of rebirth, the actual change in the solar cycle is pretty much imperceptible. The next sabbat in the progression is Imbolc and its theme is the next stage of rebirth— reemergence. At this point in the year, even when a thick blanket of snow may cover the land and spring might still feel like an eternity away, we can still see physical proof of the rebirth at Yuletide, when the sun begins to lengthen our days. By this point, we have just over forty more minutes of light than on the winter solstice.

This sabbat takes the power of the lengthening days and channels that energy into enlivening and reawakening the earth from its slumber. We too can channel this energy into revitalization and growth in our own lives

★ Imbolc Light Potion* ★

The potion for Imbolc offers us the power of the waxing light and the energy of new beginnings.

Items Needed

   2 cups water

   2 tablespoons chamomile

   1 tablespoon honey

   ½ teaspoon coriander

   ½ teaspoon sage

Charge the ingredients to connect to Imbolc and brew in the usual manner. Once cooled, the potion is strained and is ready to drink.

))●((

The following brew helps to release warmth and subtle light energy into the area to help connect with the sabbat's power.

★ Imbolc Earthfire Brew* ★

The ingredients in this brew offer a steady yet gentle energy to warm and renew, awaken and enliven, and help shift the atmosphere to the proper vibration for the holiday.

Items Needed

> 2 cups water
>
> 1 tablespoon sage
>
> 1 tablespoon chamomile
>
> 1 tablespoon sunflower seeds
>
> 2 teaspoons rosemary
>
> 3 bay leaves

Empower the ingredients to connect to the emerging power of the earth and sun that is the energy of Imbolc and brew in the usual way. This brew can be used outdoors to create a circular boundary or indoors by the hearth or on the stove to radiate its power to the home.

Ostara

When the hours of daylight have grown and reached an almost equal balance with those of the night, and the orbit of the earth has caused the sun to shine directly over the planet's equator, the spring equinox has arrived. This is the energy of balance toward growth; the delicate time when we can feel the scales tip in the favor of increase and expansion. The power of this sabbat can assist all forms of magic related to attraction, expansion, gathering, or growth.

★ Spring Green Potion* ★

The potion for Ostara gives us a greater alignment to the attraction, expansion, and growth energies available at this time.

Items Needed

  2 cups water

  1 tablespoon sage

  1 tablespoon thyme

  2 teaspoons oregano

  2 teaspoons basil

Charge the herbs to connect with the power of Ostara and the magic of balance toward growth; brew in the usual way. Once cooled and strained, this potion is ready to drink.

((●))

The brew featured for Ostara is deeply attuned to the energy of growth found within this shift from winter to spring. The magic of this mixture is one of unfolding potential. The power can be harnessed to enhance celebration as well as any magic focused on new projects, growth, or increase of any kind.

★ Ostara Energy Brew ★

This brew is packed with a surge of springtime energy and helps create an awareness of and greater connection to the waxing earth energy present at this time of year.

Items Needed

2 cups water

1 tablespoon benzoin

1 tablespoon thyme

1 tablespoon radish greens

1 tablespoon oregano

Empower the herbs to connect to Ostara and brew in the usual manner. Once cooled, this brew can be used the same way as the other sabbat brews, either to help create an outdoor circle or kept indoors to radiate its influence throughout the area.

Beltane

One of the most ancient days of power, the Beltane sabbat is often said to be second only to Samhain in significance and magic. Beltane is the opposite day to Samhain; it is its counterpart and the doorway to the light half of the year. This day is an important time when, much like at Samhain, the access between realms is greater and there is magic in the air. Whether this sabbat is celebrated on May's

Eve (April 30), May Day (May 1), when the full moon is in Scorpio, or when the sun is positioned at 15 degrees Taurus (astrological Beltane) or on another date makes little difference, as the power of this sabbat covers most of the season. The underlying theme for Beltane is growth in all forms.

★ Bright Fire Potion ★

The potion for this sabbat helps to focus and enhance our personal power as well as attune us to the overall energy of the holiday.

Items Needed

    2 cups water

    1 tablespoon woodruff

    1 tablespoon rose petals

    1 teaspoon hibiscus

    1 teaspoon passionflower tea

    1 teaspoon peppermint

    Sweetener (sugar, Stevia, or honey), to taste

Empower herbs to connect with the power of Beltane and brew it up in the usual way. Once cooled and strained, sweeten if desired and the potion is ready to drink.

((●))

The brew for Beltane is filled with bright, passionate energy that exemplifies moving from the dark half of the year into the light.

★ Beltane Garden Brew ★

Floral and herbal scents bring renewed vigor and power of the deep earth energy found at this time.

Items Needed

> 2 cups water
>
> 1 tablespoon yarrow
>
> 1 tablespoon woodruff
>
> 1 tablespoon white willow bark
>
> 1 tablespoon white heather

Charge the herbs with proper intent to connect with the energy of Beltane and brew in the usual manner. After the brew is complete, it can be used indoors or outdoors to bring additional Beltane magic.

Midsummer

The summer solstice marks the absolute peak of solar power to the earth and the longest day and shortest night of the year. The light and heat of the sun are celebrated with the knowledge that as we have reached the peak, the decline is also initiated. An underlying theme of this sabbat is paradox: though the energies of both the zenith and the shift downward are present now, the holiday's main focus is on growth, heat, and light.

★ Midsummer Power Potion* ★

This potion for the summer solstice aligns us to the sabbat's beneficial aspects; we can channel this energy for healing or prosperity.

Items Needed

> 2 cups water
>
> 1 tablespoon rosemary
>
> 1 tablespoon sage
>
> 1 tablespoon thyme
>
> ½ teaspoon summer savory
>
> Sweetener (sugar, Stevia, or honey), to taste

Empower the herbs to connect with the bright solar energy of midsummer and brew in the usual way. Remove from heat and allow the cauldron to cool, then strain the liquid and sweeten as desired. The potion is now ready to drink.

))●((

The brew for the summer solstice is filled with the light, heat, and vibrancy that are the hallmarks of the solar cycle's peak. Count on this brew to fill the area with this magical moment's radiant power.

★ Midsummer Fire Brew ★

The ingredients for this brew are a potent blend of herbs, flowers, and a powerful resin that charges the finished product with summertime magic.

Items Needed

- 2 cups water
- 1 tablespoon gardenia
- 1 tablespoon dragon's blood
- 1 teaspoon basil
- 1 teaspoon chives
- 1 teaspoon chervil

Empower the herbs to connect with the energy of the summer solstice and brew in the usual manner. Again, this brew can be used to help create an outdoor circle or kept indoors to help charge the atmosphere with the proper energy.

Lughnasadh

The magic and power of Lughnasadh are related to harvest, passage, and sacrifice. Hopefully, people have worked hard to cultivate and nurture whatever is needed to survive the coming months; now is the time to reap those rewards. This is the beginning of the harvest season and we must work hard and quickly to preserve what we have built in order to maintain the resources that will be needed to survive and hopefully thrive during the barren months of the dark half of the year. Though much of the focus at this time is on harvest (literal or symbolic) another theme is on games and competitions to demonstrate our wit, skill, and bravery.

★ First Harvest Potion* ★

The potion for Lughnasadh gathers and concentrates the holiday's light and power to help us embody the sabbat's energies.

Items Needed

1 cup water

1 black tea bag

¼ cup blackberry juice

¼ cup raspberry juice

½ cup apple juice

Empower all the ingredients with the energy of Lughnasadh. Simmer the water in the cauldron, and once the water begins to steam, remove it from heat and steep the tea bag in the water for five to ten minutes. After this, remove the tea bag, add the juices, and stir to blend. The potion is now ready to use.

))●((

This brew recipe filled with the power of the first harvest delivers that energy back to us so that we may celebrate with joy and reverence.

★ Grains of Lughnasadh Brew* ★

This brew recipe is the single exception in this book regarding consumption—all the ingredients are edible (though I can't say the liquid would taste good on its own). Once the grains and bay leaves are strained out, they can be added into a harvest meal such as a rice or barley salad to help charge it with the energy of Lughnasadh. Of course, if you choose to do this, the grains should be added into a meal before cooking it, as they will need to be cooked longer than for this brew.

Items Needed

2 cups water

1 teaspoon barley

1 teaspoon brown rice

1 teaspoon cracked wheat

3 bay leaves

Charge the grains and bay leaves with the energy of Lughnasadh and brew as usual. Once the brew has cooled and been strained, it is ready for use indoors or outdoors.

Mabon

Though we have reached another time of balance in a similar fashion to Ostara, the coming of the autumnal equinox signals that the balance is tilted toward decline. On this equinox, daytime and nighttime are essentially equal in length but from this point on until the winter solstice, the hours of night slowly overtake those of day. Mabon is the central harvest festival and has come to be known by many as the "Witches' Thanksgiving," since many Witches take this opportunity to give thanks for the bounty of the harvest and the richness of life. After all, whether or not any of us are connected directly to farming or even gardening, we all are inextricably linked to the earth's growing cycle. To many, myself included, the autumn equinox immediately brings to mind thoughts of apples, squashes, grapes, potatoes, fresh herbs, soups, and pies (since the weather is beginning to become cool enough to bake again) and finding the first pumpkins of the year.

★ Autumn Shift Potion* ★

The potion for Mabon helps to draw in and concentrate the autumn energy to fill you with the spirit of the season.

Items Needed

½ cup water

5 fresh sage leaves

1 cinnamon stick

3 whole cloves

1 cup apple juice

½ cup pomegranate juice

Empower all the ingredients to connect to the power of autumn and simmer the sage, cinnamon, and cloves in the water over low heat. Once the water begins to bubble, turn off the heat and allow it to cool. Once the water has cooled completely, strain it and add it to a large cup along with the juices, stirring to blend. The potion is now ready.

★ Autumn Feeling Brew* ★

The brew for Mabon is an earthy blend of spices and fruits that release an autumn energy and helps to align us with the energy shift taking place on this sabbat.

Items Needed

   2 cups liquid (apple cider or water)

   1 orange, cut into wedges

   1 apple, cored and chopped

   1 teaspoon cinnamon

   ¼ teaspoon nutmeg

Charge the fruits and spices to connect to the power of Mabon and brew in the usual way. This brew can be kept on the stove and water added as needed to keep the autumn energy radiating in the home as long as desired. It can also be used outdoors if preferred.

Esbats

"Esbat" is almost certainly a fairly modern word, but its meaning has changed and expanded over the years, depending upon who you ask. Some lean toward the idea that an esbat is specifically a full moon ceremony, while others use the term for any lunar-focused ritual regardless of the moon phase. Still others use the term to denote any meeting of Witches whether for ritual, magic, or teaching purposes. The potions featured here will encompass the main lunar phases when a ritual is held.

New Moon Esbat

There are two types of new moon—the astronomical and the visual. The astronomical new moon occurs when the moon cannot be seen in the sky because it is traveling (from our vantage point) in the same area as the sun. Most Witches refer to this as the dark moon. The visual new moon is the day shortly after the astronomical new moon when the lunar crescent can first be seen in the evening sky. This time is marked by some with ritual usually focused on the renewal of the lunar cycle. The potion for this day is centered on growth, increase, and beneficial magic.

★ New Moon Potion* ★

Items Needed

   1 cup water

   1 lemon, seeded and sliced

   ½ cup sliced cucumber

   1 tablespoon honey

   ¼ teaspoon lemon zest

   1 cup white grape juice

Empower each of the ingredients to capture the energy of the waxing new moon and brew the first four ingredients in the water in the usual way. After the potion has cooled and been strained, stir in the white grape juice. The potion is now ready to drink.

★ New Moon Brew ★

This brew can be used to energize the atmosphere with lunar energy and also to wash and cleanse talismans for the new moon or abundance. Again, since sandalwood is endangered, it is a good idea to substitute it for something else. An appropriate replacement for the sandalwood is the herb calamus as it is aligned with the moon and carries a similar vibration. It is also one of the first herbs I ever used magically and I've found it to be reliable.

Items Needed

2 cups water

1 tablespoon golden raisins

2 teaspoons turmeric

2 teaspoons sandalwood (or calamus)

½ teaspoon poppy seeds

Empower the ingredients and brew in the usual way.

Full Moon Esbat

The full moon is commonly associated with Witches, whether due to an understanding that most Witches are on some level attuned to lunar energies and often hold rituals during this phase or simply from the long-standing stereotype of an evil "witch" flying on a broomstick past a huge full moon. In any case, Witch and full moon; the connection is strong. Sometimes, depending on tradition or inclination, a "standard" esbat ritual is observed and other times eclectic or spontaneous ritual is performed with a wide variety of practice. This potion for the full moon can be incorporated into any type of ritual and brings more magical energy to the proceedings.

★ Esbat Energy Potion ★

Items Needed

> 2 cups water
>
> 1 tablespoon rose petals
>
> 1 tablespoon thyme
>
> 1 tablespoon yarrow
>
> 1 teaspoon mugwort
>
> 1 teaspoon eyebright
>
> Sweetener (sugar, Stevia, or honey), to taste

Empower the herbs to help draw in lunar magic and brew in the usual way. Once cooled, strain the potion into a chalice and sweeten as desired.

★ Full Moon Brew* ★

This brew is excellent to empower the working area with lunar vibrations, thereby enhancing the esbat ritual. It can be used outdoors to encircle the area or indoors to release its power.

Items Needed

> 2 cups water
>
> 1 tablespoon thyme
>
> 1 tablespoon rosemary
>
> 1 tablespoon coconut flakes
>
> 1 lemon, seeded and sliced

Charge the ingredients for the full moon and brew in the usual manner. If using outdoors, allow to cool and then strain before use.

Dark Moon Esbat

The dark moon is just after the extremely waning crescent can no longer be seen; it is the astronomical new moon. It is considered to be the culmination of the waning lunar period and is essentially the dark twin to the full moon.

★ Lunar Darkness Potion* ★

This lunar potion for the dark moon gathers the energy inward to strengthen and nurture our foundations to help us rebalance before the waxing time of the moon returns.

Items Needed
- 1 cup water
- 1 tablespoon rosemary
- 1 teaspoon vanilla extract
- ¼ teaspoon ginger
- ¼ teaspoon cinnamon
- 1 cup Concord grape juice

Charge each of the ingredients to help draw in the power of the dark moon and brew the first four ingredients in the water in the usual way. Once the potion has cooled and been strained, stir in the grape juice. The potion is complete.

★ Dark Moon Brew* ★

This brew can be used to enhance the energy of the ritual area in a manner similar to the full moon esbat brew.

Items Needed

> 2 cups water
>
> 2 tablespoons chopped lettuce heart
>
> 1 tablespoon coconut flakes
>
> 1 tablespoon rosemary
>
> 1 tablespoon vanilla extract

Charge the ingredients to draw in the power of the dark moon and brew in the usual manner. If using outdoors, allow the brew to cool and strain it before using.

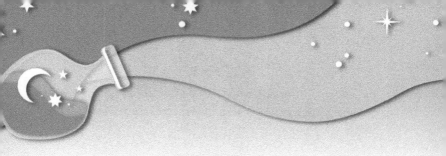

Chapter 10
POTIONS AND BREWS FOR THE ELEMENTS

Given the wide range of herbs, flowers, and other plants across the world, we have an incredible variety of options when it comes to boosting our magic with the power of potions and brews. Different herbs, flowers, and trees have different natural alignments with other aspects of nature, which is how we have come to discover the effective formulas for magical recipes. For example, roses are much more attuned to love and the element of water than, say, green beans (air) or wormwood (fire). With this in mind, there are myriad recipes for herbal creations that channel the energy of the four elements: earth, air, fire, and water.

Earth

The energy of the earth element is grounding, stable, practical, and relates to the magic of growth, nature, meditation, long-term prosperity, and protection.

★ Elemental Earth Potion ★

Items Needed

1½ cups water

2 tablespoons chopped beet

1 teaspoon mugwort

½ cup black cherry juice

Charge the ingredients to help channel the earth element and brew in the usual way. Once the potion is cooled and strained, it is ready to drink. This potion can be used to bring grounding and stability in times of excitement or stress. In such cases, the following spell may be of help.

★ Spell of Grounding Renewal ★

This spell is a magical enhancement to traditional grounding work and helps to clear away stress and anxiety.

Items Needed

1 cup prepared Elemental Earth Potion

A place to sit and meditate

If possible, find a comfortable, safe spot outdoors where you won't be disturbed. If this spell needs to be conducted indoors, it is best to use a comfortable chair with a small table nearby. To begin, sit and hold the cup of potion with both hands. Focus on your intention to ground and release stress and/or anxiety and take sips of the potion. After you have finished the potion, set the cup down and close your eyes. Feel the drink's energy blending with your own, bringing you in deeper connection to the earth. Feel as though your body is becoming heavy and sinking downward slightly until you've merged with the earth itself.

Once a solid connection is felt, sense a feeling similar to a mild magnetism, drawing the stress and anxiety down out of your body and into the land where its energy will be neutralized and recycled to greater purpose. Allow a more stable earth power to replace the stressful energy in your body so that a strong sense of calm and stability is felt. When you feel balanced and content, say this spell to seal the magic:

Harsh vibration cast away,
released to the earth to neutralize and ground;
my spirit fortified, come what may,
restored, renewed and stability found.

Mentally release the solid connection to the earth by beginning to feel lighter until you no longer feel joined to the land and affirm to yourself that your energy is secure. You may now open your eyes. The spell is complete.

★ Elemental Earth Brew ★

Items Needed

>   2 cups water
>
>   1 tablespoon pine needles
>
>   1 tablespoon patchouli
>
>   1 tablespoon barley

Empower the ingredients to channel the earth element and brew in the usual way. Once cooled and strained, the brew can be used to encircle the outside of the home for protection, added to the bathwater, or poured into a witch bottle for this same purpose. To protect the inside of a home—especially useful in cases where encircling the outside of the building is not an option—this modern spell can be used.

★ Earth Brew Spell of Home Protection ★

Items Needed

>   1 unused spray bottle, at least 2 cup
>   (16 fl. oz./~475 mL) capacity
>
>   1 culinary funnel
>
>   2 cups Elemental Earth Brew

Using the funnel, pour the strained brew into the spray bottle then attach the spray nozzle. Starting at the front door and moving from room to room in a clockwise fashion, spritz each room lightly with the spray, taking care to avoid spraying anything that could be damaged by the brew. The rooms don't have to be soaked, just spray a bit as if the brew was an air freshener spray. As you spray each room, say the following:

> *Power of earth, protect this space,*
> *freed from danger, happy and warm;*
> *keeping safe in this place,*
> *I seal this home from all harm.*

After every room has been protected, return to the front door, open it and give one spritz just outside the home to complete the protection. The spell is done.

Air

The energy of air is releasing and invigorating. The air element relates to the magic of the mind, intelligence, communication, learning, and travel.

★ Elemental Air Potion* ★

Items Needed

2 cups water

1 tablespoon anise seeds

1 tablespoon lemongrass

2 teaspoons oregano

½ teaspoon rosemary (optional)

1 tablespoon pure maple syrup

Empower each ingredient to channel the air element and brew in the usual way, reserving the maple syrup to add to the finished potion. Once cooled and strained, add the syrup. The potion is now ready to drink. This potion can be used to enhance clarity and focus and to boost the power of any magic related to the element of air. The optional inclusion of the rosemary is for those times when this potion is used specifically to aid studying, learning, remembering, and understanding,

★ Enhanced Learning Spell ★

Items Needed

1 cup of Elemental Air Potion

Study materials (such as the books you need to read or a computer)

While taking sips of the potion, look over what you need to study and envision yourself rapidly understanding and retaining the information. When you have strongly built up this intention, say the following:

Elemental air, unlock my mind,
helping me to learn, information unsealed;
my goal is reached and with ease I find
new knowledge is gained, remembered, revealed.

Finish any remaining potion in the cup and the spell is complete. Now it is time to start studying.

★ Elemental Air Brew ★

Items Needed

2 cups water

1 tablespoon dandelion

1 tablespoon lavender

1 teaspoon mint

3 clovers

Charge the herbs to channel the power of air and brew in the usual manner. Once the brew has cooled, strain it and it is ready for use. This brew can be used in the bath, a witch bottle, as an anointing liquid for elemental talismans, or to rub the temples or forehead to improve thinking. A small bit of the cooled brew can be used to water house-plants and help enliven their ability to add extra magic into the atmosphere as in the following spell.

★ Plants of Power Spell ★

Items Needed

2 cups cooled Elemental Air Brew

Houseplants

Beginning in the living room of the home and moving through each room (that has a houseplant) in a clockwise manner, water each plant with a small amount of the potion while repeating the following words:

Witch's brew of magical air,
charge this plant with enhanced ability;
to release their innate mystical flair,
filling this space with their unique energy.

The spell is complete. This spell can be repeated on a monthly basis so that the plants continue to radiate a higher degree of their individual magical properties, making your home a more magical place.

Fire

The energy of fire is expanding, radiating, consuming, releasing, generating, and transformative. The fire element relates to the magic of expansions, growth, passion, willpower, determination, conflict, aggression, and war.

★ Elemental Fire Potion ★

Items Needed

2 cups water

1 black tea bag

1 sprig peppermint

¼ teaspoon orange zest

¼ teaspoon grated fresh ginger

1 dime-sized slice ginseng (optional)

Charge all of the ingredients to channel the power of fire and brew in the usual way. Once the potion is cooled to the desired level, strain it and sweeten to taste. This potion can be consumed to increase energy and drive, prior to magical ritual as an overall power-booster, and to strengthen resolve and willpower.

★ Fire Potion Pick-Me-Up Spell ★

If you are experiencing a lack of drive, whether a feeling of self-doubt regarding whether you can achieve a goal or generally feeling burnt out or uninspired, this spell can help to reinvigorate your inner strength and determination.

Items Needed

1 cup prepared Elemental Fire Potion

Notebook and pen

Sip the potion from the cup and think about what you wish to accomplish. Envision yourself being filled with the energy, inspiration, and desire to succeed. When you have finished the potion, say the following:

> *Potion of fire, bring to me*
> *increased drive and energy;*
> *from disinterest and doubt I am freed*
> *my desire restored to achieve and succeed.*

To complete the spell, brainstorm some ideas to help you reach your goal and write them down in the notebook.

★ Elemental Fire Brew ★

Items Needed

    2 cups water

    1 tablespoon juniper berries

    1 tablespoon oak leaves, crushed

    1 tablespoon mullein

    5 cloves garlic

This brew can be used to break hexes or illness, and can be added to bathwater or a witch bottle. Empower the ingredients to channel the fire element and brew in the usual manner. Once cooled, strain the brew. It is ready for use. Another alternative: charge a heavy black or gray candle to represent the problem condition, and set it inside a cauldron or bowl. Pour the brew around it, as in the following spell.

★ Trouble Extinguisher Spell ★

Items Needed

    1 cauldron or bowl

    1 sturdy gray or black candle (that will fit in the cauldron)

    Elemental Fire Brew

Charge the candle to represent the hex, illness, or other trouble by holding it in your hands and mentally sending the problem into the candle. Place the candle into the cauldron and pour the brew around it, being careful not to wet the wick or overflow the pot. Light the candle and say the following:

> *Candle's flame and fire brew,*
> *when fire meets water the battle is won;*
> *let this trouble now undo,*
> *the harm is extinguished, a new start has begun.*
> *Elemental power set me free,*
> *as I will, so mote it be.*

When the candle burns down so far that the liquid extinguishes it, the magic is activated and the spell is complete.

Water

The energy of water is contracting, insulating, securing, bonding, and at times destabilizing. The water element relates to the magic of love, intuition, psychic work, emotion, dreams, sleep, and spirituality.

★ Elemental Water Potion ★

Items Needed

> 2 cups water
>
> 1 tablespoon catnip
>
> 1 tablespoon chamomile
>
> 1 tablespoon spearmint
>
> 1 teaspoon lemon juice
>
> 1 teaspoon sugar

Empower the ingredients to channel the power of elemental water and brew the herbs in the water. Once the potion is cooled to the desired level and strained, add the lemon juice and sugar. The potion is now ready to drink. It can be used to help soothe the nervous system as well as to aid intuitive and psychic work. It can also work as a mild sleeping potion when taken before bedtime, such as in the following spell for pleasant sleep.

★ Sweet Dreams Spell ★

Items Needed

    1 cup Elemental Water Potion

Pour a cup of the potion just before bed and hold it with both hands. Envision yourself having a peaceful night's sleep filled with pleasant dreams. Breathe gently into the cup to infuse it with your intention. When you are ready, say this spell:

> *Magical water bring to me,*
> *restful sleep and harmony;*
> *with pleasant thoughts, my slumber is filled,*
> *sweet dreams I'll have, by my free will.*

Drink the potion, then lie down in bed and have a good night. So shall it be.

★ Elemental Water Brew ★

Items Needed

    2 cups water

    1 tablespoon bladderwrack seaweed

    1 tablespoon willow leaves

    1 tablespoon yarrow

Empower the herbs to channel the element of water and brew in the usual manner. Once the brew has cooled and been strained, it is ready for use. This brew can be used in sea magic of all kinds; added to witch bottles for love, intuition or self-esteem; and a small amount can be added to the bathwater for these same intentions.

★ Witch Bottle for Love ★

Items Needed

Wide-mouth bottle with cork (or canning jar and lid) with at least a 2 cup (16 fl. oz/~475 mL) capacity

Lock of hair or nail clippings

Elemental Water Brew

Envision that this bottle's power will bring new love into your life. When this visualization is strong, add your hair or nail clippings into the bottle and then pour in the brew. Once the bottle is full, seal it. Hold the bottle in both hands and say the following:

> *Element of water, with loving energy,*
> *let this bottle be now filled;*
> *bringing new romance to me,*
> *for good of all and by free will.*

The spell is complete. Keep the bottle in a place where you can see it often but it won't be noticed by others, such as on a shelf in your closet or somewhere near your bed.

((●))

While the main focus thus far has been on water-based potion and brew recipes, the next part shifts gears slightly to look into other magical recipes that could also be considered types of potions: magically charged soups, anointing oils, and magical ointments you can make in the cauldron.

Part 3
BEYOND WATER: OTHER MAGICAL MIXTURES

It has been my intention to provide a solid book of potions and brews to close a gap that I believe has existed in the magical community for some time now. Readily available recipes for water-based, cauldron-bubbling, drinkable, usable, magical potions and useful, practical, easy-to-prepare brews are much more rare than they should be, in my opinion. That said, I am also including a few recipes for other concoctions in the interest of making this work's scope more complete. The recipes for magical soups, anointing oils, and ointments given in the following chapters can also be cooked up in the cauldron; although none of the oils or ointments featured should be consumed, they are all useful and relatively simple to make.

Additionally, oils and ointments are often called potions because they are magical mixtures used by Witches and other magical people. Their inclusion in a book of potions thus makes sense. Soups are great fun to make in a cauldron, and to empower them with magic really does turn them into an unusual and fun type of potion. While all these recipes can be created in a cauldron, a separate pot used only for food is recommended for the edible recipes in this section to avoid any possibility of the flavor of stronger herbs used in some of the other mixtures to find their way into the food.

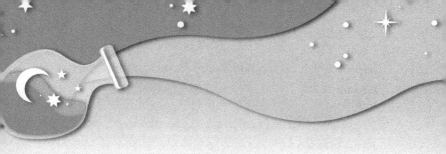

Chapter 11
CAULDRON COOKERY

Though most of us know how to cook or at least reheat things like soups and sauces, exploring magical versions of these dishes can give us not only new magical recipes to try but also a new perspective on the ones we already use. So many ingredients that we use in everyday cooking have powerful magical energy within them. Culinary herbs, of course, are carriers of potent magical energies for a variety of intentions. Foods such as garlic and onions have strong healing and protective powers. Whether a simple broth for good health or a thick, creamy soup for healing, there are many recipes to try for a touch of food magic.

Chicken soup is a classic healing food; one of my previous books has my own recipe for it. What follows here is an updated version. Paired with crusty bread and a healing potion, this soup should have a sick person feeling better in no time at all.

★ Furie Healing Chicken Soup* ★

Items Needed

2 boneless, skinless chicken breasts

1 large onion, chopped

3 cloves garlic, minced

2 chicken bouillon cubes

5 cups water

1 stalk celery, cut lengthwise and chopped

2 carrots, chopped small

1 tomato, chopped

1½ cups pasta, ideally non GMO

Salt, to taste

¼ cup parsley

1 bay leaf

Empower each ingredient for healing. Cube the chicken and cook the pieces for two to three minutes, turning at least once on each side in a lightly oiled frying pan with the onion and garlic. Turn off the heat and drain off the excess oil. Next, in a large stock pot add the bouillon cubes and water along with the remaining ingredients, excluding the chicken. Cook for about fifteen minutes until the vegetables and noodles are tender. Now, add the chicken, garlic, and onion mixture and cook for a few more minutes, stirring to blend the flavors. Remove from heat, discard the bay leaf, and serve hot.

If protection from harm or malevolent forces is a concern, this next recipe is a good one to try. It is very necessary to like the taste of garlic to eat this though. You can add noodles and/or meat to this if you wish, but the original recipe is a thickened broth soup.

★ Cheesy Garlicky Protection Broth* ★

Items Needed

1 full bulb garlic, cloves separated and peeled

1 pint water

3 bay leaves

1 teaspoon sage

½ teaspoon rosemary

½ teaspoon thyme

2 egg yolks

⅓ cup grated parmesan cheese

¼ cup olive oil

1 pint milk

Salt and pepper to taste

Empower each of the ingredients for protection. Finely mince the peeled garlic cloves and add them to a stock pot along with the herbs and water. Simmer this for 20 minutes on low (adding a tablespoon of water at a time if needed,) and then remove from heat. Next, whisk the egg yolks, cheese and oil together. Add one cup of the herb broth and whisk again. Return the stock pot to the stove and stir in the milk. Whisk in the cheese mixture over low heat until it has thickened. Remove from heat again and serve hot with bread or crackers.

(((●)))

Turning to the subject of love, two classic Italian dishes: tomato, basil and leek soup and pesto sauce can be combined to create a potent and delicious dish filled with the magical energies for love and romance.

★ Romantic Tomato and Pesto Soup* ★

Items Needed

2 tablespoons olive oil, divided

1 large onion, chopped

3 cloves garlic, minced

1 carrot, chopped

1 potato, peeled and chopped

2 16-ounce cans whole peeled tomatoes

4 cups vegetable broth

Salt, to taste

1 large leek, cut lengthwise and chopped

Chop all the vegetables and crush the tomatoes reserving the juice. Empower the ingredients for love and romance. Heat 1 tablespoon of the oil in a medium stock pot and add the onion, garlic, carrots, and potatoes, stirring frequently and cooking for 5 minutes. Next, add the tomatoes with their juice, the vegetable broth, and salt to taste. Bring everything to a boil then reduce the heat and simmer for 20 minutes or until the vegetables are tender.

While this part of the soup is simmering, wash the chopped leeks and then sauté them in a pan with the remaining tablespoon of oil, cooking until tender. After the soup has finished simmering, turn off the heat and puree the soup using a stick blender or a hand mixer. Once the soup is smooth, add the leeks and cover. Now it is time to prepare the pesto.

★ Pesto* ★

Items Needed

⅓ cup olive oil

¼ cup grated parmesan cheese

¼ cup parsley

1 garlic clove, minced

½ cup fresh basil

1 teaspoon salt

¼ teaspoon nutmeg, ground

Empower the ingredients for love and then puree everything together in a blender on medium until combined.

Swirl the pesto in the soup and then reheat it for five minutes before serving.

((●))

This next recipe is a super easy and quick soup which is magically aligned for empowering new projects and shifting your energy toward growth and prosperity. It has a mix of fresh vegetables and powerful herbs to create a very magical concoction.

★ Vegetable-Herb Prosperity Soup* ★

Items Needed

3 large potatoes, chopped

2 carrots, diced

1 large zucchini, halved and sliced thick

1 cup macaroni pasta

2 teaspoons thyme

2 teaspoons oregano

1 teaspoon salt

1 teaspoon sugar

4 cups water

2 cups prepared spaghetti sauce

Empower each of the ingredients for growth and prosperity. Add all of the ingredients to a stock pot, except for the spaghetti sauce. Simmer the soup until the pasta and vegetables are tender. Then add the spaghetti sauce and continue to simmer, stirring frequently until thickened slightly. Serve warm, ideally with big hunk of French bread or good crackers.

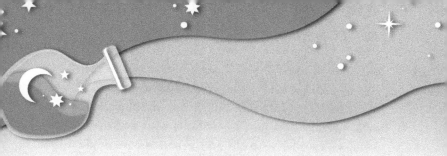

Chapter 12
OILS

Magical oils are frequently considered a type of potion because they are often specially crafted mixes of herbs and other powerful ingredients, just like their water-based counterparts. The small collection of recipes in this chapter uses the method of herbal-infused oils, which is similar to the method of water-based potion making: the herbs are warmed in the oil over low heat until their aroma is released, the cauldron is removed from the heat, allowed to completely cool, and the oil is then strained and bottled for use. Infused oils are thus mixtures in which a base oil and plant materials are heated or steeped together so that the plants' properties are extracted into the oil. By contrast, essential oils are distilled extracts of the plants' own volatile oils (usually without the addition of any base oils) and as such are highly concentrated creations. Either type of oil can be used to anoint spell candles or talismans. They can also be used to dab on the wrists, third eye area, and back of the neck to absorb their energy into the body. For safety's sake, essential oils should be diluted with a carrier oil such as jojoba or olive to avoid skin irritations. A couple drops of oil can also be added to herbal sachets to enhance their power.

Aside from using my preferred method, infused magical oils, there is another method for creating blends using essential oils. I have done it in the past but have found the cauldron simmering method to be more in tune with my needs. To my mind, it is less expensive, more personal, and (some would say) more traditional to personally create infused herbal oils rather than using ready-made products from a store, an option that of course wouldn't have existed centuries ago. That said, the cauldron method is more involved and a bit messier; if you would prefer to convert these recipes to essential oil preparation, all that is needed is to choose an appropriate carrier oil and convert measurements accordingly.

Carrier Oils

Carrier oils are usually plant-based oils mild enough in volatility, scent, and energy to provide a means of diluting strong essential oils so that they last longer, do not irritate the skin, and allow more than one oil to be blended in a recipe. The most common carrier oils are: apricot kernel oil, grapeseed oil, jojoba oil, and olive oil.

Apricot kernel oil: This oil is pressed from apricot pits. Due to its mild nature, it makes a good carrier or base oil for stronger scents. The primary magical associations for apricot are love and sex, so this oil makes a good base for magical mixtures of those intentions.

Grapeseed oil: This oil is pressed from the tiny seeds found in old-fashioned seeded grapes. Grapes have lunar associations, but are also magically aligned with fertility, money magic, and strengthening the mind. This carrier oils provides an excellent base for any relevant mixtures.[3]

Jojoba "oil": This is an interesting one … probably the best overall carrier oil, it is not in fact an oil but rather a liquid type of plant wax. Jojoba is not prone to turning rancid as the other oils do, and it is considered fairly inert so it can form an equally good base for oil blends of any intention.

Olive oil: This oil is a fiery oil that is aligned with peace, perhaps paradoxically. It is also magically linked

---

3. Scott Cunningham, *Cunningham's Encyclopedia of Magical Herbs* (St. Paul, MN: Llewellyn Publications, 1991), 130.

to fertility, healing, sexuality, and protection and provides a good base for recipes of these types. Unlike the other oils, this one is strongly scented, which may alter the overall fragrance of the finished product. "Lighter" olive oils are now readily available which are a lot less fragrant and can be used as carrier oils.

Once you have chosen the carrier oil, the measurements can be converted. In general, if using an essential oil, the ratio is 10 to 14 drops of essential oils per ¼ cup of carrier oil. The recipes in this book make ½ cup of finished oil, so that would need to be doubled. Without getting too particular over exact measurements, a good general rule of thumb is to change a ¼ teaspoon of an herbal ingredient to 1 (or 2) drops of essential oil. For example, if a recipe called for ¼ teaspoon of cloves, that would be changed to 1 or 2 drops of clove essential oil. In keeping with this conversion, 1 teaspoon of dried herbal ingredient would then be 4 drops of essential oil, and 1 tablespoon of herbal ingredient (which is 3 teaspoons) would instead be 12 drops of essential oil.

A complete example is presented here using my recipe for Money Oil.

Money Oil (Infused Version)

½ cup sunflower oil

1 teaspoon basil

1 teaspoon patchouli

½ teaspoon ginger

Money Oil (Essential Oil Version)

¼ cup sunflower oil

4 drops basil essential oil

4 drops patchouli essential oil

2 (or 3) drops ginger essential oil

As you can see, the essential oil version only uses ¼ cup of the carrier oil, which in this case is sunflower oil. If you wish to make the full half-cup recipe, the essential oil amounts can be doubled so that the resulting oil is properly scented and empowered. Your measurements do not have to be too exact; essential oils are heavily concentrated and highly scented, so the finished product really depends on individual oils and personal preference. Another consideration for the making of magical oils is whether to use a fixative, whether through the simmering or essential oil methods.

Fixatives

Fixatives are either herbs or special mixtures that help keep oils fresh and retain the quality of their fragrance. Some common fixatives I have used include copal, frankincense, orris root, and tincture of benzoin.

Copal: A resin from plants in the *Bursera* family, there are more than three hundred known varieties. Most of these varieties have associations with love and purification magic, so copal can be used as a fixative in oils of these types. A pinch of the ground resin added to the oil is all that is needed.

Frankincense: Well known for centuries, this resin is associated with spirituality purification, consecration, and protection and is a fine fixative in oils of these types. My personal use of frankincense has fallen off due to the trees' endangerment as a result of high demand; it is difficult to justify using it unless absolutely necessary. If you choose to use this one, add only a pinch of the ground resin to the oil mixture.

Orris root: This is the root of different iris flowers. It is used for love magic and protection against evil, and it makes a good fixative in oils of these types. A pinch of the ground root added to the oil mixture will suffice. You may have to stir this one well with a spoon, as ground orris root has an almost cornstarch-like consistency different from heavier resins that blend more easily.

Tincture of benzoin: Benzoin is the resin from trees of the *Styrax* family and is often used in incense making (like frankincense) as a fixative and base.

The tincture can either be purchased or made quite easily at home: add some benzoin powder to ethyl alcohol and let it steep for a week or two in a dark place. Associated magically with purification and prosperity, this was the first fixative I ever used when making oils. I have found that it works quite well for oils of all magical intentions.

Only a small amount of fixative is needed to preserve the oils, no more than ¼ teaspoon, added to the oils after blending is complete. In addition to the ones listed in this chapter, most of the potion recipes throughout the book can be converted into oil recipes except for the ones involving juices or alcohol. To convert, simply eliminate the water and replace it with ½ cup oil.

Anointing

If using any of the magical oils on yourself or others, it is a good idea to anoint some of the primary pulse points such as the wrists or the inside bend of the elbows so that the energy of the oil is properly absorbed. It is also common to anoint the soles of the feet, back of the knees, wrists, heart area, back of the neck, and third eye area to fully infuse the body with the oil's magic. However, it is often sufficient to anoint the wrists, back of the neck, and third eye only.

Traditions for anointing candles vary, but I like to anoint from the top down when working magic to bring something and from the bottom up on the candle when working magic to be free of something. Your approach to anointing an object depends upon the nature of the object. Above all, it is never a good idea to anoint a fragile or antique item with oil as it may damage the item. Any object that would be ruined is best left unanointed. But for something such as an amulet, talisman, or stone, a small amount of oil can be dabbed onto the fingers and then rubbed onto it to charge it with power. Now that the preliminary steps have been covered, let us move on to some recipes.

★ Cleansing Oil ★

This oil can be used to anoint oneself or objects (if safe or practical to do so) in need of cleansing. For a person, anoint the soles of the feet, the back of the knees, the wrists, third eye area, and the back of the neck with a very small amount of oil at each point.

Items Needed

> ½ cup olive oil
>
> 1 tablespoon elder flowers
>
> 1 tablespoon oak leaves
>
> 1 teaspoon rosemary
>
> ¼ teaspoon fixative (optional; see Fixatives, page 209)

Charge the ingredients for cleansing and heat everything together in the cauldron over low heat until you can smell the herbs in the air. Remove from heat and allow the oil to cool completely before straining and bottling for use.

★ A Universal Esbat Oil* ★

This oil is an easy and effective means of charging oneself with lunar energy to create a stronger alignment to the power of any esbat.

Items Needed

½ cup grapeseed oil

2 teaspoons lemon zest

1 teaspoon coconut flakes

1 teaspoon cucumber seeds

1 teaspoon poppy seeds

¼ teaspoon fixative (optional; see Fixatives, page 209)

Empower the ingredients and heat over low in the usual way. Once cooled, strained, and bottled, expose the oil to the light of the moon overnight but make sure to keep it out of sunlight.

★ Healing Oil ★

This mixture helps to revitalize the energy of the body to speed healing and recovery. With this one, it is best to anoint all the major points: soles of the feet, back of knees, wrists, heart, back of neck, and third eye to fully infuse the person with a strong amount of healing energy.

Items Needed

½ cup olive oil

1 teaspoon nettle

1 teaspoon rosemary

1 teaspoon thyme

1 teaspoon peppermint

3 bay leaves

¼ teaspoon fixative (optional; see Fixatives, page 209)

Empower the ingredients for healing and make in the usual way. Cool, strain, and bottle for use.

★ Love Oil ★

This light floral oil carries a wonderful, loving vibration. For a heavier, somewhat masculine-specific element to it, use tincture of benzoin as the fixative. For a more feminine-specific vibration, use ground orris root as the fixative.

Items Needed

½ cup apricot kernel oil (or olive)

1 teaspoon rose

1 teaspoon apple peels

½ teaspoon coriander

½ teaspoon lavender

¼ teaspoon fixative (optional; see Fixatives, page 209)

Empower the ingredients for love, and heat the oil in the usual way. After the oil has cooled, strain and bottle for use.

★ Good Luck Oil* ★

Bright and spicy, this oil can be used to add energy to good luck charms and even lightly dabbed on the corners of lottery tickets or paper money. If you use them on lottery tickets, be very careful so as not to ruin them; just a tiny amount of oil will do.

Items Needed

½ cup corn oil

1 teaspoon allspice

1 teaspoon nutmeg

1 teaspoon orange zest

½ teaspoon mace

¼ teaspoon fixative (optional; see Fixatives, page 209)

Empower the spices and zest for luck and correct choices. Make in the usual manner. Once cooled and strained, bottle for use, ideally in a green or royal blue bottle.

★ Money Oil ★

Heavy, earthy, and powerful, this money blend will attract prosperity in all its forms when dabbed onto paper money or used in candle magic and other spellwork.

Items Needed

½ cup sunflower oil

1 teaspoon basil

1 teaspoon patchouli

½ teaspoon ginger

¼ teaspoon fixative (optional; see Fixatives, page 209)

Empower the ingredients for money and make in the usual way. Once the oil has cooled, strain and bottle in a gold, green, or clear bottle.

★ Protection Oil* ★

The ingredients for this protection oil are super easy to obtain; you might already have them in your kitchen. Despite the fact that they are ordinary cooking herbs, each ingredient carries a strong protective energy that makes for a very effective combination.

Items Needed

½ cup olive oil

1 teaspoon basil

1 teaspoon sage

1 teaspoon oregano

¼ teaspoon fixative (optional; see Fixatives, page 209)

Charge the herbs for protection and make in the usual manner.

★ Psychic Power Oil ★

This oil helps to unlock the latent psychic abilities we each possess. The back of the neck and third eye area on the forehead are the two anointing points that should receive most of the focus when applying this mixture.

Items Needed

½ cup grapeseed oil

1 teaspoon lemongrass

1 teaspoon yarrow

½ teaspoon anise seed

¼ teaspoon fixative (optional; see Fixatives, page 209)

Empower the ingredients for psychic ability, and make the oil in the usual way. Store the cooled and strained oil in a dark blue, purple, or silver bottle.

★ A Universal Sabbat Oil ★

This recipe presents a few unusual circumstances. The first is the issue of using sandalwood and frankincense, as both are becoming increasingly endangered. If you wish to avoid these two ingredients, I've added two suitable alternative ingredients: cedar and pine needles. Though the resulting oil will be a bit different, the energy will be quite similar, just as effective, and properly attuned to sabbat power. The second thing to consider is whether to use a fixative since the original recipe has two ingredients which are themselves fixatives. If you like, choose another option from the list to use as a fixative in this recipe.

Items Needed

½ cup olive oil

¼ teaspoon powdered frankincense (or 1 teaspoon snipped pine needles)

1 teaspoon powdered myrrh

1 teaspoon powdered benzoin

1 teaspoon sandalwood (or 1 teaspoon cedar)

¼ teaspoon fixative (optional; see Fixatives, page 209)

Empower the ingredients and heat the oil, frankincense (if using), myrrh, and benzoin together, stirring the mixture until the resins have completely melted into the oil. At this point, add the sandalwood or cedar (and pine if using) and warm over very low heat until you can smell the scent in the air. Remove from heat and allow it to cool completely. Once cooled, strain and bottle for use.

⊂⊂●⊃⊃

Beyond oils is another type of magical product that can be cooked up on the stove in our cauldrons—an ointment or salve. Ointments are great homemade magical products that can be used for a variety of magical intentions. These are examined in the following chapter.

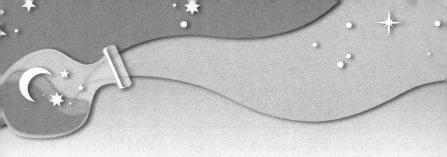

Chapter 13
OINTMENTS

Ointments or salves are relatively easy and useful items to make at home. And like all the other magical concoctions in this book, they can be cooked up right on the stove in your cauldron. There are variations in ointment recipes; for example, some are made using lard or vegetable shortening while others use oils and beeswax. I have seen other recipes made using already prepared lotions and skin creams but have not personally tried these methods, so I cannot speak to their effectiveness.

The first ointment in this chapter does not actually use any of the previously described methods but creates a protein-rich facial cream to reveal beauty, basically as a nighttime facial mask.

★ Beauty Ointment* ★

All of these ingredients are readily available at the supermarket. If possible, make this ointment with organic ingredients for a more effective product. This recipe yields one application of ointment but can be stored overnight if needed.

Items Needed

> 2 teaspoons coconut oil
>
> 1 egg yolk
>
> 1 tablespoon olive oil
>
> 1 teaspoon honey

Heat the coconut oil in the cauldron just until it melts. Remove from heat and allow it to cool slightly. Mix the remaining ingredients together with the coconut oil to form a paste, and scoop into a clean jar. Charge the ointment with the intention that it will reveal the truest form of your beauty for the highest good. This ointment is best kept in the refrigerator until you are ready to use it.

To use: Wash your face, pat dry and then apply the ointment, massaging your face gently. Do this before bed every night for seven nights. After this initial timespan, the ointment can then be applied once per week.

⊃⊃●⊂⊂

The majority of the remaining ointment recipes in the chapter all use a mixture of oil and wax to achieve a proper consistency. One of the primary reasons for choosing the use of an ointment versus using a magical oil is that they transport well. If you are attending a ritual and need to carry supplies to a distant location, a thicker substance is better transported than a messy oil. I've had more than one bottle of oil leak in a tote bag in my time, but unless the heat of the day is truly unbearable, ointments usually keep their consistency. And if that isn't a good reason to use these recipes, another is that even though there are oils in the recipes, the ointments have a less oily and greasy feel when applied to the skin. As well, they are easier to apply due to the thickness. One downside to ointments is the somewhat more difficult task of cleaning out your cauldron after making an ointment compared to making an oil, because soap is generally not advised when cleaning seasoned cast iron.

Removing Ointment Residue from a Cauldron

To effectively clean your cauldron after making an ointment (or an oil for that matter), rewarm the empty pot just to the point where anything left in the cauldron begins to melt. Remove it from the heat and stuff it with wadded up paper towels. Using a pot holder to steady the cauldron, carefully wipe out the pot with the paper towels, using more if needed. After you have soaked up as much of the ointment remains as possible, allow the cauldron to cool until you can handle it. Once cooled, rinse the cauldron well in warm water and wipe it out with a soft sponge, but do not use soap. After the rinsing, dry the cauldron using more paper towels or an absorbent dish towel. If you notice any residue, another option is heating some water in the cauldron to melt the remains and then pouring it down the drain. Again, dry the pot with towels afterward.

ᑕᑕ●ᑐᑐ

With the important mundane considerations taken care of, let us turn again to the magic. This first oil- and wax-based ointment is a version of a classic—a flying ointment, originally a mix of poisonous herbs steeped in a fat and then applied to the body to induce a type of flight most often said to be astral projection. This version does not rely upon deadly ingredients to produce its effects, so there is considerably less danger in its use.

★ Flying Ointment (Nontoxic) ★

This ointment will aid the practice of astral projection without any of the poisonous substances found in the traditional Witch's flying ointments of the past.

Items Needed

> 6 tablespoons vegetable oil
>
> 1 tablespoon dittany of Crete
>
> 1 tablespoon mugwort
>
> 1 teaspoon cinquefoil
>
> ½ teaspoon mace
>
> 3 tablespoons beeswax

Empower the ingredients for astral projection. Heat the herbs in the oil until you can smell their scent in the air. Remove from heat and allow the oil to cool. Once the oil has cooled, strain it and return it to the cauldron. Reheat the oil, this time adding the wax. Melt the wax in the oil, stirring to blend. Once the wax has melted, remove the cauldron from heat and let cool completely. Once the ointment has cooled, spoon it into a jar and it is ready to use.

To use: Anoint all of the usual points on the body (soles of the feet, back of knees, etc.) and sit or lie down in a comfortable position and relax. Envision lifting out of your body. One technique you could try would be to mentally construct an etheric double of your body floating over yourself, connected to you with a thin energy cord to your third eye or the top of your head. Attempt to transfer your awareness into this double in a similar fashion to focusing awareness on a single point of your body, such as how aware you become of your fingertips when searching for a light switch in a dark room. With practice, this awareness shift becomes more fully realized and longer lasting, a great help to facilitate astral travel. Another technique is to develop a feeling of lightness and to "push" your consciousness out of your body via the third eye chakra. This can often feel like squeezing through a narrow window or porthole. Personally, I prefer the etheric double technique, but some people have quicker success with this method. In any case, these are not the only methods to try. If you'd like to study up on astral travel, it is a fascinating pastime. Richard Webster's *Astral Travel for Beginners* (Llewellyn, 2002) is a solid starter guide to the practice.

★ Healing Ointment ★

This ointment helps strengthen the body's ability to heal itself in times of illness or injury.

Items Needed

6 tablespoons vegetable oil

1 tablespoon rosemary

1 tablespoon peppermint

3 bay leaves, crushed

1 clove garlic, minced

3 tablespoons beeswax

Empower the ingredients for healing and heat the herbs and garlic in the oil until you can smell their scent in the air. Remove from heat and allow the oil to cool. Once the oil has cooled, strain it and return it to the cauldron. Reheat the oil, this time adding the wax. Melt the wax in the oil, stirring to blend. Once the wax has melted, remove the cauldron from heat and let cool completely. Once the ointment has cooled, spoon it into a jar and it is ready to use.

To use: This ointment makes an excellent rub for muscle or joint pain. In times of illness, it can be rubbed onto the chest like a vapor rub and can also be anointed at the usual points to bring power into the body. That said, I would avoid the third eye anointing point; when I'm feeling ill, I don't want anything on my face. Two other words of caution: If you are feeling nauseated, it is best to avoid use of this ointment, as the garlic and/or peppermint aromas might cause problems; secondly, do not apply this ointment to burns, wounds, or broken skin. If you have these injuries, you can still apply the ointment to other points on the body to help yourself heal energetically.

★ Hex-Breaking Ointment ★

This recipe provides a nice ointment empowered with the ability to neutralize any harmful energy sent your way, whether through an actual hex or random harsh energy unconsciously directed at you from others such as difficult coworkers, angry motorists, et cetera.

Items Needed

6 tablespoons vegetable oil

1 tablespoon vetiver

1 tablespoon pine

1 teaspoon ginger

1 teaspoon peppermint

3 tablespoons beeswax

Empower the ingredients for purification and hex removal. Warm the oil in the cauldron and add the herbs, heating until you can smell them in the air. Remove the cauldron from the heat and allow the oil to cool enough so that it can be strained. Once strained, return the oil to the cauldron and reheat it, this time adding the beeswax. Slowly melt the wax into the oil, stirring to mix. As soon as the wax is melted, remove the pot from the heat once again. Once it has cooled, spoon the ointment into a jar for use. This mixture can be used to anoint the usual points on the body to infuse its power into yourself. It is especially helpful to anoint yourself just before bedtime so that any harmful energy can be neutralized during sleep.

★ Love Attraction Salve ★

The ingredients of this ointment carry strong loving, attraction and sensual energies and can be a powerful enhancer to any magic aimed at finding a romantic partner of any type.

Items Needed

6 tablespoons vegetable oil

2 tablespoons lavender

½ teaspoon ginger

½ teaspoon cardamom

3 tablespoons beeswax

¼ teaspoon vanilla extract

Empower the ingredients for love and attraction. Warm the oil in the cauldron, and add the herbs, heating until you can smell the herbs in the air. Remove it from the heat and allow it to cool enough so that it can be strained. Once strained, return the oil to the cauldron and reheat it, this time adding the beeswax. Slowly melt the wax into the oil, stirring to mix. As soon as the wax is melted, remove the pot from the heat once again. Once cooled, stir in the vanilla extract and spoon the ointment into a jar for use.

To use: Before spell-work designed to attract love, anoint the body at the usual points to boost the spell's power.

It can also be used before going on dates to heighten loving vibrations.

★ Protection Salve ★

This ointment can be used to anoint the body for personal protection and also to anoint amulets to help them keep their magical charge.

Items Needed

6 tablespoons vegetable oil

2 teaspoons juniper berries

2 teaspoons peppermint

1 teaspoon pennyroyal

1 teaspoon vervain

3 tablespoons beeswax

Empower the ingredients for protection. Warm the oil in the cauldron and add the herbs, heating until you can smell the herbs in the air. Remove it from the heat and allow it to cool enough so that it can be strained. Once strained, return the oil to the cauldron and reheat it, this time adding the beeswax. Slowly melt the wax into the oil, stirring to mix. As soon as the wax is melted, remove the pot from the heat once again. Once it has cooled, spoon the ointment into a jar for use. Much like the hex-breaking ointment, this mixture can be used to anoint the body just before sleep to keep you safe from harm.

★ Psychic Power Ointment ★

Vision, clarity, communication, and retention of information received via psychic work are all boosted with the use of this ointment.

Items Needed

6 tablespoons vegetable oil

2 teaspoons mugwort

2 teaspoons yarrow

1 teaspoon lemongrass

3 star anise pods, crushed

3 tablespoons beeswax

Empower the ingredients for psychic ability. Warm the oil in the cauldron and add the herbs, heating until you can smell the herbs in the air. Remove it from the heat and allow it to cool enough so that it can be strained. Once strained, return the oil to the cauldron and reheat it, this time adding the beeswax. Slowly melt the wax into the oil, stirring to mix. As soon as the wax is melted, remove the pot from the heat once again. Once it has cooled, spoon the ointment into a jar for use. This salve is best used to anoint the third eye, wrists, and back of the neck prior to divinatory and psychic work to enhance your innate abilities.

★ Sabbat Ointment ★

This ointment is similar to a sabbat oil in that it can be used to anoint the body to attune to the extra energies of these days of power.

Items Needed

   6 tablespoons vegetable oil

   1 teaspoon myrrh

   1 teaspoon sandalwood

   1 teaspoon cinnamon

   ½ teaspoon dried lemon zest

   ½ teaspoon dried orange zest

   3 tablespoons beeswax

Empower the ingredients to connect to the sabbats. Warm the oil in the cauldron and add the herbs, heating until you can smell the herbs in the air. Remove the cauldron from the heat and allow it to cool enough so that it can be strained. Once strained, return the oil to the cauldron and reheat it, this time adding the beeswax. Slowly melt the wax into the oil, stirring to mix. As soon as the wax is melted, remove the pot from the heat once again. Once it has cooled, spoon the ointment into a jar for use.

To use: Anoint the usual points on the body prior to sabbat rituals to more fully attune to the energy of the holiday and to enhance your ability to draw upon these powers in magical work. It can also be used more passively by anointing the body at the beginning of the day to continually draw upon the sabbat energy even when ritual cannot be conducted. This is very useful for those times when a rite must be postponed due to scheduling conflicts, unusual circumstances, or weather concerns but you still want to do something to attune to the holiday.

★ Vision Salve ★

While the psychic power ointment recipe above helps to boost general psychic power and the interpretation and retention of information received, this formula is more specifically focused on enhancing the power of psychic vision, clairvoyance.

Items Needed

1 tablespoon angelica

1 tablespoon mugwort

1 teaspoon chicory

½ cup vegetable shortening

Grind and empower each herb and blend them together with the shortening. Heat the mixture in the cauldron in the same manner as with magical oils. Remove from heat. When the mixture has cooled a bit but the shortening is still liquid, strain and bottle the ointment for use. To use the ointment, dab a small amount on the third eye area of the forehead and a little on the wrists and back of the neck when engaging in psychic or divinatory work to boost the clairvoyant abilities.

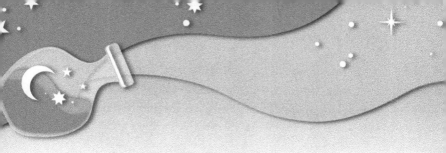

CONCLUSION

It is my ardent wish that this work showed readers how useful the nearly lost art of potion and brew making can be in the magical world. I would be very happy to see a revival in the practice that has us all demanding food-safe cauldrons at reasonable prices. It might be a fantastical hope, but I would love to know that real magical potions could finally take their place alongside the other herbal preparations such as incenses and oils so that this art form endures and remains relevant in the twenty-first century and beyond; may its power never be lost.

Hopefully, I have been able to properly convey my joy and enthusiasm for cooking up potions in a cauldron; it is truly one of my favorite aspects of Witchcraft. Potions and brews are a fun and surprisingly practical form of magical work. Whether bubbled up in a cast-iron cauldron over an open flame, cooked up in a modern coffee maker, or any way in between, these recipes can all be used either on their own or to enhance other forms of magic. Happy potion making, and may all of your magic bring you joy and fulfilment.

Blessed Be,
Michael Furie

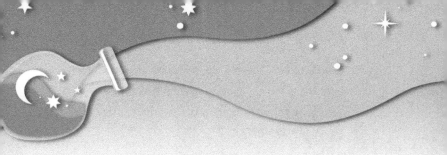

Appendix 1
MAGICAL COLOR CORRESPONDENCES

Colors in Magic

Use these colors when choosing candles, fabrics, or inks to help draw in the proper energies in alignment with your magical intentions.

Black: grounding, absorbing, protection, Pluto and Scorpio energy

White: learning, projecting, all-purpose, Uranus and Aquarius energy

Red: passion, love, sex, conflict, force, war, Mars and Aries energy

Orange: communication, direction, Mercury and Gemini energy

Yellow: intellect, divination, persuasion, sun and Leo energy

Green: growth, healing, abundance, love, plants, Venus and Taurus energy

Blue: happiness, peace, soothing, influence, luck, Jupiter and Sagittarius energy

Indigo Blue: psychic ability, deep thought, sleep, Saturn and Capricorn energy

Purple: spirituality, meditation, higher energy, power, authority

Pink: love, friendship, self-esteem, Venus and Libra energy

Silver: dreams, moon magic, intuition, goddess energy, moon and Cancer energy

Gold: strength, success, prosperity, god energy, sun and Leo energy

Gray: neutralization, stalemate, clearing, balance, Mercury and Virgo energy

Brown: animals, grounding, Saturn energy, earth energy

Copper: love, beauty, Venus energy

Opalescent Color: Neptune and Pisces energy

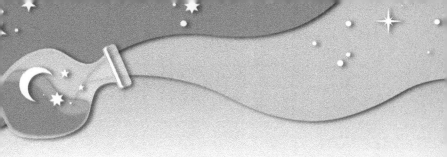

Appendix 2
INGREDIENT TABLE
OF CORRESPONDENCES

Here is a listing of herbs, fruits, grains, and other ingredients in this book's recipes. I have included as complete a listing of items as possible as a handy reference table for creating your own mixtures and for discovering the magical potential of other recipes found in books or online. Each ingredient is listed by name with corresponding element, planet, polarity and magical uses included; some items have more than one association. The polarities listed will be along the yin/yang axis which I find less limiting than the "masculine/feminine" dynamic frequently used in herbal reference works. Not every listing contains information on planet, element, or polarity; some items have a universal alignment.

Ingredient	Element	Planet	Polarity	Magical Uses
Alfalfa	Earth	Venus	Yin	Money, poverty protection
Allspice	Fire	Mars	Yang	Money, luck, healing
Almond (nut and oil)	Air	Mercury	Yang	Money, prosperity, wisdom
Angelica	Fire	Sun	Yang	Exorcism, visions, healing
Anise	Air	Jupiter, Pluto	Yang	Protection, meditation, purification
Apple	Water	Venus	Yin	Love, healing, faery magic
Apricot	Water	Venus	Yin	Love
Barley	Earth	Venus	Yin	Love, protection
Basil	Fire	Mars, Pluto	Yang	Love, banishing, wealth
Bay leaf	Fire	Sun	Yang	Clairvoyance, purification, protection
Bean	Air	Mercury	Yang	Protection, banishing
Beet	Earth	Saturn	Yin	Love
Benzoin	Air	Sun	Yang	Purification, prosperity
Blackberry	Water	Venus	Yin	Healing, protection, money

Ingredient	Element	Planet	Polarity	Magical Uses
Black cohosh	Fire	Pluto	Yin	Courage, love
Blueberry	Earth	Venus	Yin	Protection, warding
Caraway	Air	Mercury	Yang	Protection, lust
Cardamom	Water	Venus	Yin	Love, lust
Catnip	Water	Venus	Yin	Love, happiness
Cayenne	Fire	Sun	Yang	Hex breaking, passion
Chamomile	Water	Sun, Neptune	Yang	Sleep, peace, money, love
Cherry	Water	Venus	Yin	Fertility, love, divination
Chervil	Air	Mercury	Yin	Spirit contact, wisdom, repels evil
Chicory	Air	Sun	Yang	Luck, favor, frugality
Chili pepper	Fire	Mars	Yang	Hex breaking, passion
Chives	Fire	Mars	Yang	Banishing, protection
Cinnamon	Fire	Sun	Yang	Spirituality, love, success
Cinquefoil (five finger grass)	Fire	Jupiter	Yang	Multi-purpose

Ingredient	Element	Planet	Polarity	Magical Uses
Clove	Fire	Jupiter	Yang	Banishing, protection, love, money
Club soda	Water	Moon	Yin	Releasing energy, uniting elements
Coconut	Water	Moon	Yin	Protection, moon magic
Coffee	Fire, Water	Mars, Neptune	Yin	Energy, clarity, divination
Copal	Fire	Sun	Yang	Purification, love
Coriander (cilantro)	Fire	Mars	Yang	Love, lust, healing
Cramp bark	Water	Saturn	Yin	Healing, protection
Cranberry	Fire, Water	Mars, Venus	Yin	Protection, love, wine substitute
Cucumber	Water	Moon	Yin	Healing, fertility, moon magic
Cumin	Fire	Mars	Yang	Anti-theft, protection, banishing
Dandelion	Air	Jupiter	Yang	Divination, wishes
Dill	Fire	Mercury	Yang	Money, lust, protection
Dittany of Crete	Water	Venus	Yin	Astral projection
Elder	Water	Venus	Yin	Exorcism, healing

Ingredient	Element	Planet	Polarity	Magical Uses
Eyebright	Air	Sun	Yang	Psychic and mental power
Fennel	Fire	Mercury, Uranus	Yang	Protection, healing, purification
Fenugreek	Air	Mercury	Yang	Money
Fir	Earth	Jupiter	Yang	Healing, clarity
Frankincense	Fire	Sun	Yang	Spirituality, protection
Gardenia	Water	Moon	Yin	Love, peace, spirituality
Garlic	Fire	Mars	Yang	Protection, banishing, healing
Ginger	Fire	Mars	Yang	Power, love, money
Ginseng	Fire	Sun	Yang	Love, healing, protection
Grape	Water	Moon	Yin	Fertility, abundance, moon magic
Grapefruit	Fire	Jupiter, Saturn	Yang	Purification, healing
Hazelnut (filbert)	Air	Sun	Yang	Wisdom, protection, luck
Heather	Water	Venus	Yin	Protection, luck
Hibiscus (tea)	Water	Venus	Yin	Lust, love
High John the conqueror	Fire	Mars	Yang	Money, success, love

Ingredient	Element	Planet	Polarity	Magical Uses
Holly	Fire	Mars	Yang	Protection, luck
Honey	Earth	Venus	Yin	Love, binding, healing, prosperity
Hops	Air	Mars	Yang	Healing, sleep
Horehound	Air	Mercury	Yang	Protection, healing
Horseradish	Fire	Mars	Yang	Banishing exorcism, purification
Huckleberry (can substitute for blueberry)	Water	Venus	Yin	Purification, luck, hex breaking
Hyssop	Fire	Jupiter	Yang	Purification, protection
Ivy	Water	Saturn	Yin	Protection, healing
Juniper	Fire	Sun	Yang	Protection, healing
Kelp	Water	Jupiter	Yin	Protection, sea magic
Lavender	Air	Mercury	Yang	Protection, love, sleep
Leek	Fire	Mars	Yang	Protection, banishing, love
Lemon	Water	Moon	Yin	Purification, love, moon magic
Lemongrass	Air	Mercury	Yang	Psychic awareness

Ingredient	Element	Planet	Polarity	Magical Uses
Lettuce	Water	Moon, Saturn	Yin	Sleep, chastity, moon magic
Licorice root	Water	Venus	Yin	Love, lust
Lime	Fire	Sun, Uranus	Yang	Purification, healing, love
Mace (nutmeg)	Air	Mercury	Yang	Divination, mental powers
Maple (syrup)	Air	Jupiter	Yang	Love, healing, calm, binding
Marjoram (substitute with oregano)	Air	Mercury	Yang	Love, protection, money, healing
Millet	Earth	Jupiter	Yang	Money, luck, healing
Mint	Air	Mercury	Yang	Money, healing, purification
Mugwort	Earth	Venus	Yin	Psychic power, protection
Mullein	Fire	Saturn	Yin	Protection, healing
Myrrh	Water	Moon	Yin	Protection, healing
Nettle	Fire	Mars	Yang	Protection, exorcism
Nutmeg	Air	Mercury	Yang	Luck, money, love, healing
Oak	Fire	Sun	Yang	Money, health, protection

Ingredient	Element	Planet	Polarity	Magical Uses
Oat	Earth	Venus	Yin	Money, abundance
Olive (fruit and oil)	Fire	Sun	Yang	Healing, peace, fertility, luck
Onion	Fire	Mars	Yang	Protection, banishing, healing
Orange	Fire	Sun	Yang	Love, luck, money
Oregano	Air	Mercury	Yang	Love, protection, money, healing
Orris	Water	Venus	Yin	Love
Paprika (*Capsicum*)	Fire	Mars	Yang	Magical booster, creativity
Parsley	Air	Mercury	Yang	Purification, lust
Patchouli	Earth	Saturn	Yin	Money, lust, fertility
Peach	Water	Venus	Yin	Love, fertility
Pennyroyal	Fire	Mars	Yang	Strength, protection
Pepper (black)	Fire	Mars	Yang	Protection, banishing
Pine	Air	Mars	Yang	Healing, protection, money
Pineapple	Fire	Sun	Yang	Luck, money
Pistachio	Air	Mercury	Yang	Hex breaking
Plum	Water	Venus, Saturn	Yin	Love, protection

Ingredient	Element	Planet	Polarity	Magical Uses
Pomegranate (fruit and juice)	Fire	Mercury	Yang	Luck, fertility, protection
Poppy seed	Water	Neptune	Yin	Moon magic, love, money
Prune	Water	Venus	Yin	Healing, love
Pumpkin	Earth	Moon	Yin	Prosperity, healing, moon magic
Radish	Fire	Mars	Yang	Protection, love, lust
Raspberry	Water	Venus	Yin	Love, protection
Rice	Air	Sun	Yang	Money, fertility, protection
Rose	Water	Venus	Yin	Love, psychic power
Rosemary	Fire	Sun	Yang	Purification, protection, love
Rye	Earth	Venus, Pluto	Yin	Love, protection
Saffron	Fire	Sun	Yang	Love, healing, luck, strength
Safflower	Fire	Mars	Yang	Divination, exorcism, hex breaking
Sage	Air	Jupiter	Yang	Protection, money, cleansing

Ingredient	Element	Planet	Polarity	Magical Uses
Salt	Earth			Purification, blessing, protection
Sandalwood	Water	Moon	Yin	Protection, healing, spirituality
Sassafras	Fire	Jupiter	Yang	Healing, money
Seaweed (bladderwrack, kelp)	Water	Moon	Yin	Sea magic, protection, psychic work
Sesame (oil, seeds)	Fire	Sun	Yang	Money, opportunity, lust
Shortening (lard)				Base for salves
Slippery elm	Air	Saturn	Yin	Stopping gossip
Soy	Earth	Moon	Yin	Psychic awareness, protection
Spirits (distilled alcohol)	Fire	(Varies based on ingredients)		Offering, spirituality, purification
Squash	Air	Moon	Yin	Psychic ability, fertility, moon magic
Star anise				Psychic ability, protection, hex breaking
Stevia	Water	Jupiter	Yin	Healing, success
Strawberry	Water	Venus	Yin	Love, luck

Ingredient	Element	Planet	Polarity	Magical Uses
Sugar	Water	Venus	Yin	Love, purification
Summer savory	Air	Mercury	Yang	Healing, love, lust
Sunflower (seeds and oil)	Air	Mercury	Yang	Fertility, luck, strength
Tarragon	Air	Venus	Yin	Love, protection, purification
Tea	Fire	Sun	Yang	Money, lust, courage
Thyme	Water	Venus	Yin	Healing, energy, purification
Tomato	Water	Venus	Yin	Protection, love, money
Turmeric	Water	Moon	Yin	Purification, fertility, moon magic
Turnip	Earth	Moon	Yin	Protection, banishing
Valerian	Water	Venus	Yin	Sleep, purification
Vanilla	Water	Venus	Yin	Love, energy, lust
Vervain	Earth	Venus	Yin	Love, purification, protection
Vetiver	Earth	Venus	Yin	Hex breaking, luck, money
Vinegar	Fire			Purification, banishing, healing

Ingredient	Element	Planet	Polarity	Magical Uses
Wheat	Earth	Venus	Yin	Money, abundance, fertility
Willow	Water	Moon	Yin	Love, healing, divination
Wine (red)	Earth, Fire	Sun	Yang	Luck, happiness, love, sun magic
Wine (white)	Earth, Water	Moon	Yin	Luck, happiness, love, moon magic
Woodruff	Fire	Mars	Yang	Protection, money, success
Wormwood	Fire	Mars	Yang	Psychic power, protection
Yarrow	Water	Venus	Yin	Psychic power, love

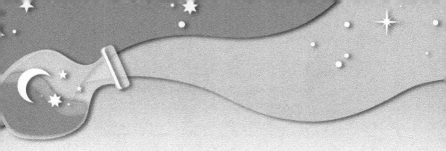

BIBLIOGRAPHY

Amaranthus. *Feasting from the Black Cauldron: Teaching from a Witches' Clan*. Green Valley Lake, CA: Pendraig Publishing, 2017.

Blair, Briana. *The Herbal Magic Correspondences Guide*. Raleigh, NC: Lulu.com, 2014.

Cabot, Laurie. *Celebrate the Earth: A Year of Holidays in the Pagan Tradition*. New York: Delta, 1994.

———. *Laurie Cabot's Book of Shadows*. Salem, NH: Copper Cauldron Publishing, 2015.

———. *Laurie Cabot's Book of Spells and Enchantments*. Salem, NH: Copper Cauldron Publishing, 2014.

———. *Power of the Witch: The Earth, the Moon and the Magical Path to Enlightenment*. New York: Delta, 1989.

Cunningham, Scott. *The Magic in Food: Legends, Lore and Spellwork.* St. Paul, MN: Llewellyn Publications, 1991.

———. *The Magical Household: Spells and Rituals for the Home.* St. Paul, MN: Llewellyn Publications, 2010.

diGregorio, Sophia. *Traditional Witches' Formulary and Potion-making Guide: Recipes for Magical Oils, Powders, and Other Potions.* n.l.: Winter Tempest Books, 2012.

Huson, Paul. *Mastering Witchcraft: A Practical Guide for Witches, Warlocks, and Covens.* New York: GP Putnam & Sons, 1970.

Illes, Judika. *Encyclopedia of 5,000 Spells: The Ultimate Reference Book for the Magical Arts.* New York: HarperOne, 2004.

Law, Donald. *Herb Growing for Health.* New York: ARC Books, 1972.

Orapello, Christopher, and Tara-Love Maguire. *Besom, Stang & Sword: A Guide to Traditional Witchcraft, the Six-Fold Path & the Hidden Landscape.* Newburyport, MA: Weiser Books, 2018.

Paulsen, Kathryn. *Witches' Potions and Spells.* Mount Vernon, NY: Peter Pauper Press, 1971.

Raven, Gwion. *The Magic of Food: Rituals, Offerings, and Why We Eat Together*. Woodbury, MN: Llewellyn Publications, 2020.

Telesco, Patricia. *A Witch's Beverages and Brews: Magick Potions Made Easy.* Franklin Lakes, NJ: New Page Books, 2001.

Webster, Richard. *Astral Travel for Beginners: Transcend Time and Space with Out-of-Body Experiences.* St. Paul, MN: Llewellyn Publications, 2002.

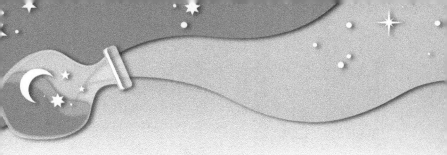

INDEX